HIGH

LOW

Buffalo

The Power of God-Centered Perspective

HIGH
LOW
Buffalo

JESSIE SENECA

High Low Buffalo
Copyright © 2022 Jessie Seneca
ISBN 978-1-961198-00-5 paperback • ISBN 978-1-961198-09-8 ebook
Library of Congress Control Number: 2022913001
Religion, Christian Life, Personal Growth

Printed in the United States of America
Published in Hellertown, PA

Copyedit Fran D. Lowe • Cover design Susan Myers • Interior design Helen Ounjian
Cover art credit: Yakovliev, Stock illustration ID:538998238

Printed in the United States of America
For more information or to place bulk orders,
contact the author or the publisher at Jennifer@BrightCommunications.net

Bright
COMMUNICATIONS
BrightCommunications.net

To my grandchildren . . .

The greatest buffalo has been becoming your Mimi!
Never did I think my heart could expand
and explode in the ways it has.
You bring one high after another and lots of fun
buffaloes into your Mimi and Papaya's lives!
I pray you will continue the tradition your
mom/Aunt Sarah began—High, Low, Buffalo

How do we live to our fullest potential, no matter what? Jessie Seneca wisely reminds us that "in every place a purpose exists." She helps us to see how our perspective frames our circumstances and invites us to take an intentional approach to make the most of every day. This book is a gift at any age in any season. We can truly encounter God in the messy, the mundane—and the miraculous moments in our lives.

Angela Donadio
Author, speaker,
and host of the Make Life Matter *podcast*

Jessie reminded me that perspective IS everything and the best is yet to come. This must-read book is filled with principles to be practiced daily. Her personal and biblical examples and challenging quotes from others challenged my perspective and reminded me that I become what controls my mind. With each practical step given and probing and reflective question asked, I gained a more positive perspective and attitude. This wonderfully inspiring book gave me the fresh eyes needed to see God's hand and plan in each high, low, and buffalo. Refreshed and ready to relaunch, I am moving forward and not backward! Thank you, Jessie.

Sally H. Hall
Author of Self-Talk

Such encouragement! It will be a blessing to all that read it. Jessie's books are always very relatable, and yet there's no fluff. This book is packed full of Scripture, biblical truths, and wisdom. There is one quotable quote and aha moment after another. I'll never view my highs and lows the same again—and I'll always keep an eye out for the buffaloes!

Mandy Hood
Executive Director, The Connection

Jessie's insight into the power of our perspective has enriched my understanding of this important topic. An incorrect perspective can lead us to disappointment, hopelessness, and despair that comes from expectations not aligned with God's truth, plan, and purpose. A God-centered perspective promotes trust, which allows us to live with hope, courage, and anticipation for all God is doing in and through us. The High, Low, Buffalo exercise causes us to be intentional about evaluating the events of our life, to look for the silver linings and lessons learned and to see how God is causing all things to work together for good. Jessie inspires us towards a deeper trust perspective. I believe all who read Jessie's book will be blessed with a God-centered perspective that will set them free from living a life of unfulfilled expectations.

Sue Landis, PHR, CPEC
Women's Ministry,
Small Business & Life Coach

Our perspective determines the trajectory and impact of our lives. In *High, Low, Buffalo* we're given biblical encouragement for shifting how we perceive life's circumstances, and how we allow them to affect us. We learn to view life through the lens of God's Word. As we do, we stop reacting from emotion and begin responding with His love, grace, and joy. *High, Low, Buffalo* will inspire life-giving conversations in your home.

Eryn Lynum
Speaker and author of 936 Pennies:
Discovering the Joy of Intentional Parenting

In *High, Low, Buffalo* you will read these powerfully repeated words: "Perspective is everything" and "One thing we can control is our attitude." We've all heard these phrases, and probably even agreed with them. However, the difference here is that Jessie Seneca, through her poignant and personal grounded-in-God's-Word writing style, presents these oft-heard phrases as encouraging and challenging life choices. Whatever life may bring us—those sweet Highs of life, those painful Lows, or those Buffaloes, with their unexpected joyful surprises and life lessons—Jessie makes it clear, as does our God, that we have a choice to make about our perspective and our responses that flow from that perspective. Will we remain stuck in a place of doubt, discontent, frustration, fear, or prideful self-reliance? Or will we humbly acknowledge, trust, and obey our God as the loving Giver of life and the ultimate, victorious Author of our story—no matter what chapters are written in our lives? Let the grace and truth written in *High, Low, Buffalo* deepen your understanding of God's love for you and the power God offers you as you choose a God-centered perspective right in the midst of whatever you are walking through—today, tomorrow and each new day!

Sylane Mack, M.S.
President of Transformed by Grace
counselor, author, international speaker

When Jessie asked me to endorse her new book, I knew it would be a wonderful book because I know Jessie. Jessie lives what she teaches—she is pure gold through and through. However, I had no idea what a truly inspirational and life-changing book *High, Low, Buffalo* would be. As I began to quickly glance through the first few pages, I found myself captivated by her thoughts and therefore slowing down and absorbing the rich truths that Jessie was sharing. If your desire is to live the life of God's dreams, *High, Low, Buffalo* just might open the windows of your heart to the ability to do so. I can't wait to buy a copy of this book for myself and for my family!

Carol McLeod
Best-selling author,
Bible teacher and podcaster

High, Low, Buffalo: The Power of God-centered Perspective challenges you to meditate, ponder, and reflect. As you look over your life, Jessie helps you celebrate the exciting moments (the highs), identify the purpose of the disappointments (the lows), and be captivated when discovering your unexpected Buffalo moments. When your perspective shifts from a worldly, defeated outlook to one clarified by a loving God, numerous unexpected blessings are revealed.

Life is filled with ups and down, births and deaths, health and wealth challenges. Jessie has compiled one of the greatest biblical resources available to help shift your perspective to one of celebration instead of sorrow. It's simple, get your copy today!

Keri Spring
Director of Digital Discipleship,
Carol McLeod Ministries

This book will help you get into the rhythm of rejoicing and reflecting, practices that are sorely needed in our noisy and negative digital world. Jessie Seneca is a faithful mentor who can help us reframe the difficulties we face. She'll show you how to notice the gifts and treasures coming from God, delivered each day with love.

Arlene Pellicane
Author of Parents Rising
and host of the Happy Home *podcast*

A positive Christian is a contagious Christian—but how do we discover positivity when life feels so challenging? With inviting storytelling, solid biblical application, and practical questions that take the reader from passive to action, Jessie introduces us to a simple yet profound answer: *High, Low, Buffalo.* This book was the encouragement I needed to start choosing my perspective—one that looks ahead with holy anticipation at all that God can and will do. With intentionality and obedience, we can choose each day to have a positive perspective and a positive influence on those around us.

Crystal Stine
Author of Holy Hustle:
Embracing a Work-Hard, Rest-Well Life
and Quieting the Shout of Should:
How a Life of Less Can Lead to More

Preface

A few years back, our youngest daughter, Sarah, introduced our family to a fun and introspective way to close out our day and times together. Welcome to our family's interactive activity of reflection. I hope you find this book helpful, inspiring, and encouraging, and that you'll have some good ol' fun with it!

We've cherished our time together as a growing family. We've laughed 'til, yes, some of us have wet our pants. Cried 'til our mascara ran. And embraced the surprises with great joy. John and I are now the proud Mimi and Papaya (Pops) to three grandsons and first granddaughter on the way. It's definitely true when you hear the saying, "If I knew it was going to be this much fun, I would have become a grandparent first." To say we are enjoying this season of life is an understatement. The activity of *High, Low, Buffalo* has taken on a whole new meaning with the addition of the grandkiddos, and we look forward to the days ahead. We know there will be days that are easier to embrace than others, but just like you, we have to take the good with the not-so-good.

High, Low, Buffalo: The Power of God-centered Perspective presents you, your family, and friends with a fun, yet purposeful, challenge to reflect and identify the good, bad, and unexpected in your day—your *high* being the good, your *low* being a disappointment or less than desired experience, and your *buffalo* being an unexpected blessing you experience. Oftentimes, we find ourselves reacting out of our flesh to what happens to us, but God calls us to something more. By seeing our moments through His eyes, we are able to adjust our perspective and appreciate the different ways He is working throughout our day. My prayer is this simple yet thought-provoking challenge of *High, Low, Buffalo,* will encourage you to do just that.

Whether doing this exercise alone or with others, my hope is that you will celebrate the highs, learn from the lows, and enjoy the buffaloes—that your perspective would grow to be one that sees your whole day as a gift from God. And please, enjoy the journey. Each day is a gift from God!

Jessie

Contents

Teach us to number our days and
recognize how few they are;
help us to spend them as we should.
Psalm 90:12 TLB

High

As you reflect on the close of each day and consider the day's findings, you may wonder if anything you did made an impact and moved you forward. Some days you may find yourself in the same rut as the day before. It begs the question, do you need to make a change, or just view life through a different lens? This is where *High, Low, Buffalo* comes in—it's time to refresh your perspective.

Whether our family is together for a day or an extended period of time, my daughter, Sarah, challenges us to share a *High, Low, Buffalo*. The *high* represents the exciting and best part of your day, with the *low* representing a disappointment or less than desired experience. The final part is your *buffalo*, or that random, unexpected blessing you experienced—a welcomed surprise. It is a fun and reflective way to close out your day, even though deciding what to share takes a good bit of consideration and intentionality. What you choose to be your *High, Low, Buffalo* is all determined by the perspective you choose to have as you reflect on your day. Perspective is everything.

1

Positivity defers you from thoughts that send you into a downward spiral. It provides a strong mindset to override the negative talk you tell yourself. A positive Christian is a contagious Christian—one who draws deep joy from Christ to draw others to Him.

After living through the COVID-19 worldwide pandemic that began in the spring of 2020, you can most likely ramble off a lot of lows, but if you look deeper, you can find the highs and some really great buffaloes. I think we all can agree that each time we enter a new year, we have no idea what it will hold, but 2020 took the cake on surprises. Never did we expect the reality of 2020. Some were paralyzed by the seclusion, while others were energized. No matter where you found yourself, life looked different, and we all seemed to be on a leveled playing field. It was an unprecedented time that required an unprecedented response—a time to get creative or remain in disappointment.

Each day, the perspective you choose to have greatly impacts your heart and subsequently your actions. Ultimately, the choice is yours. Yes, no one can make this decision for you but you!

For me, 2020 left me missing the face-to-face gatherings of women, speaking at live events, hugging friends and family, and people-filled holidays. But as I reflect specifically on this season of life and More of Him Ministries, I see many *buffaloes*. This ministry unexpectedly expanded, stretching me beyond what I thought I could do. Although we may not know when things may feel "normal" again, this life experience has left an impact on each of our lives. Regardless of what that may look like, we can continue to fulfill God's call and move forward in His strength. We must continue to move forward! It all depends on our individual perspective.

Your *high* will be different from my *high*, but it will most likely be the best part of your day or week. Some of your *highs* will transfer into life-changing, memorable moments that will impact your life and those around you. Mark Batterson, in his book, *Win the Day: 7 Daily Habits to Help You Stress Less & Accomplish More*, made this statement, "Time is measured in minutes. Life is measured in moments."[1] This is pure truth. It's the small moments that link your days, months, and years together to create your timeline.

There are days you don't feel that your actions make much of a difference, but this couldn't be further from the truth. It's in the ordinary that God uses you for extraordinary opportunities. It may not be the timing you hoped for, but God's timing is perfect. When you're obedient in the small things God requires from you, He will build upon each action to create the destiny He has marked out for you. And your ability to walk in this obedience all begins with your mindset. What perspective will you choose?

Looking back over my fifty-plus years, I have seen God's hand upon every step I took to bring me right where I am today, and each season built upon the next in God's timeline for me. It's important to appreciate each season and embrace change. Or you could find yourself sitting in a heap of lows wishing for the next season. Maybe you are in the season of:

- Wiping little faces or reading the same children's book for the millionth time.
- Serving in a ministry you thought would look different.
- Working in an unfulfilling job.
- Battling a disease and fighting for your life.
- Mourning the loss of what were once dear friendships.
- Celebrating the high you are walking through.

No matter where you find yourself, if your perspective can be one grounded in, "I want to be obedient to the Lord and become more like Him," God will use each moment, day, and opportunity to build upon the next and reveal Himself to you in ways far above and beyond what you could imagine.

May our heart's prayer be, "God, You are great, and there is none like You! Nothing or no one can compare to You. Nothing that we have heard with our ears or seen with our own eyes can stand in comparison to You. Therefore, You are great and greatly to be praised" (2 Samuel 7:22)!

Recently while reading Jon Gordon's book, *The Shark and the Goldfish*, this statement hit me like a ton of bricks: 'If you think your best days are behind you, they are. If you think your best days are ahead of you, they are."[2] Talk about perspective!

Prior to reading this statement, I was longing for the days of the past in ministry and missing what was. I thought, *If we could just go back . . .* Yes, it feels like the past was wonderful, but what if God has something new and exciting around the corner? Am I ready to have a new perspective—that God holds my days and works for my good? What perspective will you choose as you move forward in obedience?

This I know: God's on the other side of your uncertainties. Yes, it seems like we live in uncertain times. Although I still believe this is true, I am starting to accept that we all live uncertain lives. Indeed, God's truth and our eternal destiny in Christ are certain, yet many other factors in our lives are a bit unpredictable and unclear at times. It is the nature of the journey.

Recently, our pastor shared a portion of Brennan Manning's book, *Ruthless Trust*, in which his daily devotional brought the point of uncertainty home for me. He shared the story of John Kavanaugh, the noted and famous ethicist, who went to Calcutta, seeking Mother Teresa . . . and more. He went for three months to work at 'the house of the dying," to find out how best he could spend the rest of his life.

When he met Mother Teresa, he asked her to pray for him. "What do you want me to pray for?" she replied. He then uttered the request he had carried thousands of miles: "Clarity. Pray that I have clarity."

"No," Mother Teresa answered, "I will not do that." When he asked her why, she said, "Clarity is the last thing you are clinging to and must let go of." When Kavanaugh said that she always seemed to have clarity, the very kind of clarity he was looking for, Mother Teresa laughed and said, "I have never had clarity; what I have always had is trust. So I will pray that you trust God."[3]

As my pastor continued his devotional, he challenged us with these words, "There is something in all of us that always wants clarity. It is part of our sinful ego and a common expression of our insecurities. Clarity can become an idol that replaces authentic trust in God. In many ways, we would rather understand the details of the road ahead than rest in deep intimacy with the God who has promised to direct our steps."

The Bible tells us, "Trust in Him at all times, you people; pour out your heart before Him; God is a refuge for us" (Psalm 62:8). We must pour out our hearts and all they contain: praise, gratitude, worry, fear, doubt, and, yes, uncertainty. God is our in-the-moment refuge—our quick prayer receiver, but not always a divine GPS system revealing the details of each turn we might encounter one year down the road. Thus, we must trust Him at all times and watch for the buffaloes, He will surprise us with along our journey.

As I look back on the road traveled, I am thankful God didn't reveal the highs, the lows, or the buffaloes of my life in one viewing. If He had, I am not sure I could have endured. Instead, He gave me portions of my journey as He revealed His ways through each day of my life.

No matter what you are facing, He wants to be at the center of it all. He wants to be your guiding light, your deepest longing, and brightest reflection. He wants to be the *high* in your day!

> *Those who look to Him for help*
> *will be radiant with joy;*
> *no shadow of shame will darken their faces.*
> (Psalm 34:5 NLT)

Your one act of obedience may not only impact those who walk with you but also a generation that follows. In 1996, while I was sitting in the audience listening to the speakers at a Women of Faith event in my hometown, the words of a counselor who cared for me during one of my hospital stays for three months during my illness ran through my mind: *Someday you will be sharing your experience with others.* It was at that event I felt God calling me into a teaching/ speaking ministry. I didn't share this with anyone but my mother-in-law, who attended the conference with me.

Even during my battle with Cushing's syndrome, I knew there was more to life than "just" surviving. I felt that God may use my story in a way that would encourage others. At the time, it was hard to understand God's will in it all, and even when I felt His call, I didn't know what it would look like. Yet, I still trusted Him with the outcome . . . or did I?

Although I felt God's call on my life in 1996, it was a twelve-year wait until I received my first invitation to share at another church. Honestly, there were times I wondered why. *Why, God, have You not opened the door yet?* But during this twelve-year period of preparation, I would feverishly immerse myself in God's Word through multiple Bible studies, as well as work in various ministries. Each experience built on the previous one and prepared me for the open door God called me to enter through years later.

Sometimes I felt discouraged that God didn't move a little faster in the process. I wanted to hurry Him along. But through a tough lesson, God showed me that He wanted me to be willing to speak to one woman first rather than a multitude. What God wanted and what I thought were very different. Humbled by a song I was listening to while waiting to pick up my then preschooler, I heard God speak to my heart, "Are you willing to speak to one person?"

When I finally bent my knee to His plan and became willing to speak to just one person, God began His plan, not mine. What I thought would be a call to reach multitudes, God meant for an audience of one. However, today God has expanded that audience of one to a larger gathering. It is your obedience in the small things that will be the gateway for God to open doors for expanded use and greater impact.

Likewise, at times you may wonder, *Is this what God wants from me?*

His calling on my life seemed to take longer to develop than I anticipated. Yet, through the waiting, I came to know God in a deeper way. He showed me more about Himself, and I realized that the preparation time was necessary for this season of my life. If I had stepped ahead of God, it would have been a complete train wreck. I would definitely not have been prepared. Yet now, in His timing, I am walking in the fullness of His calling. I don't always know the next step, but I've learned to trust Him and just follow Him for the day ahead of me. One moment of obedience becomes a stepping stone to the pathway of God's destiny for your life—a life committed to fulfilling His call.

I share this personal story to say that God builds upon some of your darkest and lowest moments in order to accomplish His will. I know you may find it hard to embrace some of your experiences as God's plan. However, in every place a purpose exists, and it's up to you to experience this purpose to its fullest. Regardless of the situation, you can control only one thing—your attitude, which you will read about many times throughout this book. Oh, others can affect your attitude, but you get to choose how you will respond. Will you have a Promised Land attitude, or a wilderness attitude? One of expectancy and joy, or one that displays complaining and "Woe is me"?

One night while watching *Man in the Arena—The Life of Tom Brady*, a documentary about the well-known quarterback, with my husband, I was surprised how drawn into his story I became. It was not the story of football that captured me, but the close-knit family that was his foundation. Through the trials and heartaches their family went through, his one sister made a comment I couldn't shake off. As she shared about their mother's illness and cancer diagnosis, her outlook was compelling. Her approach to the situation indicated one of optimism and hope when she said, "Rather than saying, 'Why is this happening *to* me?' ask, 'Why is this happening *for* me?'" This one little word switch, *to* to *for*, can change your perspective. It goes from an infliction to a benefit, a negative to a positive—a low to a buffalo.

If you can view your disappointments as Paul did in the first chapter of Philippians, it will help you walk out the days ahead of you. Verse 12 says, "Now I want you to know, brethren, that my circumstances have turned out for the greater progress of the gospel." Like Paul did regarding his imprisonment, can you look at what you have gone through and consider it steppingstones to all God has for you in the future? Paul continues in Philippians 1:21-24:

> *For to me, to live is Christ and to die is gain. But if I am to live on in the flesh, this will mean fruitful labor for me; and I do not know which to choose. But I am hard-pressed from both directions, having the*

desire to depart and be with Christ, for that
is very much better; yet to remain on in
the flesh is more necessary for your sake.

God has kept you alive and given you opportunity for fruitful living. Yes, fruitful living! So, what are you going to do with it? Are you going to live your life to your fullest potential? Or are you going to settle for ease and comfort? Revelation 3:7 (NIV) says, "These are the words of Him who is holy and true . . . What He opens no one can shut, and what He shuts no one can open."

Aim to please God and not man. If you choose to trust God alone, you will end up right in the middle of what God has called you to for this specific time and place. "Behold, [He] will do something new, now it will spring forth; will you not be aware of it? [He] will even make a roadway in the wilderness, and rivers in the desert" (Isaiah 43:19). God can turn the lowest part of your day into a high if you allow Him.

We are not meant to live on mountaintop experiences all of our days, although the highs we encounter with God will certainly strengthen us to be able to walk through the valleys. God will be with us through the valley and give us strength to carry on. A valley is most likely between two mountains. If you are walking through a valley experience right now, be watchful, because there is a new mountain on the horizon, one God wants you to experience. The climb will be so worth it, my friend.

Psalm 23:4 reminds us of God's faithfulness to us: "Even though I walk through the valley of the shadow of death, I fear no evil, for You are with me; Your rod and Your staff, they comfort me." His rod and staff are your guide and protection. He will carry you through and walk beside you, so you will be able to laugh without fear of the future (Proverbs 31:25).

Consider Ezekiel, a prophet in the Old Testament that prophesied to the Jews exiled to Babylon because of their rebellion against God. His message was less than favorable with lamentation, mourning, and woe as the Israelites lost the presence of God among them. However, Ezekiel also prophesied of a coming restoration that would take place in the millennial kingdom. You may deem the prophecy of Ezekiel as a low, but prior to sending him to the Israelites, God revealed Himself to Ezekiel in an amazing vision of the Lord's glory through a whirlwind, fire, brilliant lights, four creatures, wheels, beautiful gems, wings, and God's presence. When Ezekiel saw it, he fell face down and heard a voice speaking: "Son of man, I am sending you to the Israelites, to the rebellious pagans who have rebelled against me" (Ezekiel 2:3).

I fully believe God gave Ezekiel this great vision and high experience prior to sending him to the wolves so he would have this glorious vision of God to carry him through some rough days ahead with a bunch of hard-headed, stiff-necked people. Aren't you thankful that God allows us to experience His presence and *highs* so that we are able to walk through the lows? Without Ezekiel's encounter with God, I often wonder if he would have been able to carry out his assignment. You and I may not experience visions as Ezekiel did, but through God's Word we are strengthened and encouraged by His promises to us. Also, there are moments in the quietness of your devotional time with Him when God reveals Himself and touches the innermost part of you that changes your attitude, commitment, confidence, and strength.

And like Ezekiel, we can move ahead with the strength of the *highs* God allows us to encounter. However, we cannot stop seeking God and stay in one particular high. We must continue to seek Him with fervency and determination to know Him deeper. And as we come into a deeper relationship with Him, He will reveal Himself to us in new and fresh ways. So, we must not put God in a box but rather expect some buffaloes in places and situations that may seem uncommon. We just need to have a willing spirit, open mind, and watchful eye for His appearance, which can come in unconventional ways as well as in the most ordinary of days.

Our highs can be defining moments if we embrace them as *kairos* moments. Ephesians 5:15-16 encourages us, "Therefore be careful how you walk, not as unwise men but as wise, making the most of your time, because the days are evil." Time can be categorized as *chronos*, which is sequential—past, present, future. In other words, it is linear, moving in only one direction. It's how humans measure time, yet God exists outside the space-time dimensions He created. The second word for time is *kairos,* and it refers to the opportune time, which characterizes Ephesians 5:16. *Chronos* counts minutes, *kairos* captures moments. It's the critical moment or the appointed time—"for such a time as this" (Esther 4:14). It's *carpe diem,* "seize the day."[4]

Seizing the day will take great intentionality. It will require you to be where your feet are—from the grocery store visit, to a well-planned vacation, and everything in between. It's about being aware of your surroundings and capitalizing on the moments you're given because you never get that time back. Ugh . . . I know what you may be thinking, *Boy, have I blown it.* Don't be so hard on yourself. I have also missed one too many opportunities.

But we can move forward, watching for opportune times and embracing the ordinary moments with a fresh intent to make a difference in the lives of people with whom God intersects our days. It may mean a slower pace of life, a more watchful eye, or having a different focused outlook. Whatever it is, we should embrace the moment and thank God for another chance to make a difference in our lives and others'. Your day's high will be the highlight of your focus, and in turn, produce a grateful heart.

Reflection Questions

1. Share any life-changing, memorable moments that impacted your life and those around you.

2. Does change energize or paralyze you? Why?

3. Are you living your life to your fullest potential? If not, what adjustments will you need to make to live a more fruitful life?

4. Do you find it difficult to seize the day? If yes, how can you change your mindset to be present where you are?

Low

L ows. We all have them. But does it mean we have to like them? If we're honest, we would rather not experience them. However, we must come to a place where we hit our nemesis head on and accept lows for what they are—a less than desirable situation. Although it may not seem like it at first, something positive can come from the experience. And if we reach deeper into the situation, there is a wider lesson learned through our lows. It comes from the comfort we receive from God as He gently cares for us and walks beside us through our unwelcome circumstance. Second Corinthians 1:3-4 explains the reason His comfort is for our good: ". . . the Father of mercies and God of all comfort, who comforts us in all our affliction so that we will be able to comfort those who are in any affliction with the comfort with which we ourselves are comforted by God." He doesn't let one trial that we go through be wasted. He comforts us in it, and then in turn makes us an aid of comfort to someone else.

This comfort isn't just a soothing sympathy but an added strength that makes one strong beyond his own power.

And, you most likely have heard others say, "God doesn't give you more than you can handle." This statement is probably one of the most misquoted statements from the Scriptures. I have not found this said anywhere in the Bible. God often gives us way more than we can handle— this is called life. I believe we are better served to say, "God doesn't give you more than you can handle without Him." John 16:33 (NIV) confirms this when we read, "I have told you these things so that in Me you may have peace. In this world you will have trouble. But take heart! I have overcome the world."

Because Jesus has overcome every challenge, temptation, and trial you and I will face, we have an Advocate praying for us (Hebrews 7:25), and He promises to walk through difficulties with us wherever we may go (Joshua 1:9). Perspective is everything.

A recent conversation with a radiology technician who assisted me with my MRI reminded me of some real lows in my life. Her first question was, "Have you had any surgeries?" I snickered at the question and replied, "Do you want the full monty? One brain surgery. Three lung surgeries. One chest surgery and a tubal ligation." She proceeded to ask, "Do you have any metal in your body?" Thankfully, that answer was more favorable: No! All the surgeries were due to a battle with Cushing's syndrome, with the third lung surgery as a full left pneumonectomy. Cushing's syndrome is a rare endocrine or hormonal disorder. It occurs when the adrenal glands release too much of the hormone cortisol into the body. Most Cushing tumors are located on the pituitary gland, but they can present themselves anywhere else in the body, most likely on the lung, adrenal gland, or bronchial tube.

Due to the excessive amount of cortisol in my body, I experienced many physical and mental problems throughout twenty-plus years. At the onset of my illness, I was placed in four different hospitals for nearly five months when my girls were only two and a half years and six months old. Not only did my mental state continue to plummet, but my physical symptoms also continued to worsen as I was deteriorating before our eyes.

Along with the acne came increased anxiety, depression, hair growth on my face, a hump at the top of my back, sugar diabetes, bladder loss, and thickness around my midriff. My will to live was gone. It might seem that I had one low after another, but that couldn't be further from the truth. Although I experienced many lows, I had some really great highs as well. It's all in your perspective!

Oh, believe me, there were times I wanted to stay crawled up in a ball and not face the days ahead. You have these days, too, and it's okay. You just can't stay stuck in that place. May I be honest with you? Even though some of the memories are ones I wished for another time or not at all, they became life lessons that were only captured in the secret place with God. They were memories learned through the darkness that became beacons of light for my next step. These moments of despair became building blocks for developed strength. The loss of days brought appreciation for the here and now and hope for my future. I have always felt that every day since those difficult years has been a gift.

> *"I will give you the treasures of darkness*
>
> *And hidden wealth of secret places,*
>
> *So that you may know that it is I,*
>
> *The Lord, the God of Israel,*
>
> *who calls you by your name."*
>
> *(Isaiah 45:3)*

Both hardship and adversity are a vital part of your walk with God. God's purpose is to enable you to see that He can walk on the stormy waters of your life right now. If you have a further goal in mind, you are not paying enough attention to the present time. However, if you realize that moment-by-moment obedience is the goal, then each moment as it comes is precious.[1]

The famed America jazz singer Ella Fitzgerald once sang, "Into each life some rain must fall." Even though we can't control just how much it rains, we can control one thing—our attitude as we walk through the rain. In Mark Batterson's book, *Do It for a Day: How to Make or Break Any Habit in 30 Days*, he makes the point for the purpose of rain in our lives by restructuring the saying, "Rise and shine" to "*Rain* and shine."[2] Even if we are facing difficulty, we must still arise and pop open that umbrella and let God cover us with His wings as we seek His refuge (Psalm 91:1-4). Those same wings that protect us can be the same wings we will soar on.

The rains, of course, are the challenging or low times that we experience: negative medical diagnosis, divorce, job loss, financial security, loneliness, or even just navigating the teen years as a parent or caring for an aging parent. And though it may not seem like it at first, some positive lesson can come from the experience. Please don't allow adversity to harden your heart, but instead embrace it, and become the best learner you can be as you grow from the experience.

> We each have our own individual story.
> Some have a short journey.
> Some longer.
> Some harder than the next, and some easier.

HIGH LOW *Buffalo*

Others seem to have more lows, while some, on the surface, have a smooth journey with lots of highs. Don't allow the highs of others to discourage you. Keep your eyes focused on Jesus and only be concerned with the life He's planned out for you because it's the perfect journey toward your divine future. I believe God knows what it is going to take for each one of us to be more like His Son, Jesus Christ, and He will do whatever it takes for us to arrive safely into His arms, refining and perfecting our faith along the journey.

You have probably heard the common saying, "Pull yourself up by your bootstraps." This phrase means to improve your situation by your own efforts—to succeed or elevate yourself without any outside help.[3] At the mention of this gesture, it seems courageous to dig down deep within yourself for needed strength—that is, until your strength isn't enough, and the power to withstand something challenging finds you flat on your face.

You need more than your own effort to bounce back from heartbreak, stressful situations, or exhaustion. You need something beyond *you*! You need His glorious power working in you. It's only then that you will be ready for anything because it's the strength of the One who lives in you that allows you to do all things through Him who strengthens you (Philippians 4:13). Don't allow a day to go by without asking for more of the Holy Spirit's power

22

and guidance (Luke 11:13). The Holy Spirit is the one who makes everything that Jesus did for you real in your life.[4]

No matter where you find yourself today, something has caused fatigue to grip you in one way or another. Some days are more intense than others, but no matter where you find yourself swinging on the pendulum, you crave a stamina that will carry you through. Hebrews 12:1-2 says, "Therefore, since we have so great a cloud of witnesses surrounding us, let us also lay aside every encumbrance and the sin which so easily entangles us, and let us run with endurance the race that is set before us, fixing our eyes on Jesus, the author and perfecter of faith." To run with endurance, you must first lay aside every burden such as fear, anxiety, or a hurt-filled past—anything that keeps you from doing what God wants you to do. Second, you must lay aside the sins that entangle you, including those of unbelief, lack of obedience, or any others that continue to hurt God. He wants you to run your race lean and mean, with His endurance fixing your eyes on Jesus.

Maybe you are sitting there thinking, *I have done all this, but I still need endurance to run the race set before me.* Hebrews 12:2 continues, "...who for the joy set before Him endured the cross, despising the shame, and has sat down at the right hand of the throne of God." Yes, not all fatigue is from our sin—some fatigue is the result of going where God says go and choosing to remain until God's purpose is fulfilled.

Just as Jesus needed endurance to accomplish His purpose on Earth with the cross, you will need His endurance to obey God's purpose in your life. He's providing that same endurance for you to bravely bear what's in front of you with His power and strength, not your own. John 4:34 hits this point when Jesus says, "My food is to do the will of Him who sent Me and accomplish His work." Doing the will of God was Jesus' fuel to keep going when adversity hit. It wasn't being filled physically but rather being filled spiritually that strengthened Him. The same is true for us—drawing close to Jesus, doing His will, and fulfilling His purpose for our lives should override our physical desires and strengthen us for the days ahead.

Scottish teacher and evangelist Oswald Chambers, in his devotional, *My Utmost for His Highest*, says, "God does not give us overcoming life; He gives us life as we overcome."[5] Similarly, John 10:10 says, "The thief comes only to steal and kill and destroy; but I [Jesus] came that [you] may have life and have it abundantly." No matter what low you are experiencing, Jesus can make a way, revive your spirit, and birth new life within you through the Holy Spirit as you lean into Him and His power. Through the process of *overcoming*, you meet Jesus in a deep place of need—a place of full dependence. And through your dependence on Him, you will develop a quiet sense of security and humble confidence that births a renewed life, one fully committed to Him. Put no confidence in your flesh, but have every confidence in the God who made you, called you, saved you, and keeps you. He will accomplish great things through you when you embrace your weakness as His strength and follow the Lord's guidance and trust in the promise of His confidence—not yours.

> *For the Lord will be your confidence*
> *and keep your foot from being caught.*
> (Proverbs 3:26)

Yes, life can be hard at times, but you and I can experience abundant life. If you can look at your situation through the eyes of Jesus and continue to seek first His kingdom, He will reveal Himself to you in ways you never deemed possible. And Romans 8:28 will bring vitality to your tired soul: "And we know that in all things God works for the good of those who love Him, who have been called according to His purpose." Once you're able to embrace an attitude that God is in control of your days and you entrust your life into His hands, you will be able to look at the future with trust and confidence that He goes before you.

If you and I learned anything through the 2020 pandemic, it is that we must hold our plans and life loosely within our hands. Just when we seem to think we have everything under control, God may take matters in a new direction, so we must release our plans into His grip. His Word gives us a prescription for controlling the controllable.

First Timothy 6:11-12 tells us how to control our love and pursuit for Him: ". . . pursue righteousness, godliness, faith, love, perseverance, and gentleness. Fight the good fight of faith."

We must seek His plans and not our own agenda. Yes, He gives us free will for our day. However, if He interrupts your day, your obedience will be the key to allowing Him to change the direction. Then you must trust Him with the outcome. Obedience is up to you, but the outcome is up to God. Psalm 31:14-15 will give you the confidence to know He cares for you: "But as for me, I trust in You, O Lord, I say, 'You are my God.' My times are in Your hands." Knowing your times are in His hands will unleash you to become part of the process—the process of being moldable, which will allow you to move forward in the calling He sets before you. So keep your eyes on Him. You are the clay, and He is the potter; therefore, you are the work of His hands (Isaiah 64:8).

Are you facing something that seems bigger than you? Something that feels beyond your reach? Something you need to move forward with, despite what others may think? You say, "I can't do it." Yes, you can! Remember, you can do all things through Christ who strengthens you (Philippians 4:13). It is His power, which mightily works within you (Colossians 1:29), that allows you to take the next step, even if it's a baby step. So make the move. At the end of what may seem impossible, there will be an opportunity for God to show His power working in you. Put your trust in God. He will not forsake those who seek Him (Psalm 9:10). Nothing is too big for God!

Do not despise the small beginnings, because that's where it all starts. Small beginnings are where God births ideas for grander things to come. Neil Armstrong's famous quote when stepping onto the moon for the first time has great depth, "That's one small step for a man, one giant leap for mankind." You only need to focus on the first step and then allow the steps that follow to turn into the leap. Be faithful with what is right in front of you, and the next step will be revealed in His time. Your one act of obedience may not only impact those who walk with you but a generation that follows. Your obedience is the pathway that God will work in ways far greater than you could ever imagine.

Second Corinthians 3:5-6 is pure truth: "Not that we are adequate in ourselves so as to consider anything as having come from ourselves, but our adequacy is from God, who also made us adequate." It is His adequacy. His competence. His confidence that you can tap into. "Therefore, whatever your hand finds to do, do it with all your might" (Ecclesiastes 9:10a).

Jeremiah 17:7-8 (HCSB) gives us the remedy to moving forward despite any inadequacies or doubts that arise:

> *"The man who trusts in the Lord, whose*
> *confidence indeed is the Lord, is blessed.*
> *He will be like a tree planted by water:*
> *it sends its roots out toward a stream, it*

> *doesn't fear when heat comes, and its foliage*
> *remains green. It will not worry in a year*
> *of drought or cease producing fruit."*

When we trust God with our future and find our confidence in Him, He will bless our efforts. This attitude is unlike the man who trusts in mere human effort and whose heart is turned away from Him—his life will be cursed (Jeremiah 17:6). Psalm 147:10-11 (NIV) provides the blessing that comes from those who look to God rather than man, 'His pleasure is not in the strength of the horse, nor His delight in the legs of the warrior; the Lord delights in those who fear Him, who put their hope in His unfailing love."

You and I will need to trust God when our human thoughts want to take us in a different direction. Put your confidence in God, not man. Your security in Jesus' finished work on the cross will be a strong foundation when all else seems to be crumbling around you—putting on His armor will give you the strength you need for the situation in front of you:

> *Stand firm then, with the belt of truth buckled*
> *around your waist, with the breastplate of*
> *righteousness in place, and with your feet*
> *fitted with the readiness that comes from the*
> *gospel of peace. In addition to all this, take*
> *up the shield of faith, with which you can*
> *extinguish all the flaming arrows of the evil*

> *one. Take the helmet of salvation and the*
> *sword of the Spirit, which is the word of God.*
> (Ephesians 6:14-17 NIV)

Put on His full armor and walk in the confidence of Christ. Yes, you can be a woman clothed in strength and dignity and smile at the days ahead (Proverbs 31:25). For added security, grab a friend and stand back-to-back both wearing the armor of God, and you will sense added confidence. Remember, God has kept you alive and given you opportunity for fruitful living.

What you do with the opportunities given to you is your gift back to God through your response, action, and commitment. Your reward is often on the other side of obedience. Lean into the unknown and watch God work. I want you to stop for a moment and ask yourself these few questions.

- Are you ready to take a risk?
- Do you see the value over "today" versus the mentality of an eventual "one day"?
- Does change energize you or paralyze you?
- Do you take responsibility for your life and decisions?
- Are you ready to finish what you started?
- Are you willing to do what others are not, even if that includes hard work?

Nothing is too big for God! He wants you to learn from your low moments and maybe even a failure to catapult you forward and take a new risk. Be willing to do something new with God as your co-pilot. Commit your way to Him and allow Him to determine the time and place of blessing. You will watch Him do far more above and beyond what you could ever imagine or think according to the power working within you (Ephesians 3:20).

Yes, you already have this power if you have received Jesus' love in your heart and confess Him as Lord! The Holy Spirit is a gift and has been entrusted to all who believe, not just a reward to some. You just have to access His power, step out in faith, and embrace the Holy Spirit as your friend and guide. Luke 11:13 tells us to ask for more of the Holy Spirit, and your heavenly Father will give Him to you. Stepping out with confidence will take a strength higher and stronger than yourself.

So, 'Delight yourself in the Lord; and He will give you the desires of your heart. Commit your way to the Lord, trust also in Him, and He will do it . . . . Rest in the Lord; wait patiently for Him to act" (Psalm 37:4-7). Open your eyes that you may behold the wonderful things from God's law (Psalm 119:18), which will give you a clearer perspective of the days ahead.

Reflection Questions

1. Have you ever stayed stuck in a low place? Did anything good come from it?

2. Share life lessons you learned from your low experiences.

3. Have you ever faced something that seemed impossible, but at the end of that impossible task or situation, there was an opportunity to show God's power working in you?

Three
Buffalo

Let's define "buffalo" again. A buffalo reflection represents a random or unexpected blessing—a surprise in your day. And who doesn't love a good surprise? Sometimes it's hard to decipher between your high and a buffalo because they both fall under a positive expression of gratitude. When we are surprised, whether it's good or bad, our emotions intensify. When our buffalo is something positive, we'll feel a more intense feeling of happiness or joy than we normally feel—it brightens our day and puts a smile on our face.

As I have shared the title of this book, most people understood the high and low part of one's day, but the majority of them didn't know what a "buffalo" was. Once I explained the process to them, you could see the smile on their faces, and they would say, "I am going to add this to our day's reflection." Just as those who have heard about this challenge and implemented it into their day, I hope you embrace the day's ending challenge too.

- An attitude of gratitude will bring peace and contentment into your life.
- It will put a skip in your walk.
- It will be an unspeakable joy to others.
- It will bring an added brightness to your face.

Others will wonder where your quiet confidence comes from and inquire about your joy. The secret of Jesus can be revealed to others through your example of a grateful heart. The root of your happiness will be grounded in your contentment. When you make holiness your aim, happiness and joy will follow. Joy is something you will deliberately need to choose. No one can choose it for you.

Some buffaloes are extremely recognizable, while others may need to be thoughtfully searched for. Either way, it should, for the most part, be a delight to our day. A buffalo can range from an unexpected visit from our bestie, a creative gift sent in the mail or dropped at our front door, to a kind action shown by an unforeseen companion. You get the gist of this—the buffalo will be different for each one of us, but nevertheless, a highlight in our day.

However, sometimes life takes you in unexpected places. And in these least expected places, your heart will be exposed to your emotions and attitude. Will you have a buffalo attitude, or will you reject the surprise? Maybe what seemed to be a low at first glance becomes a buffalo. With time you're able to embrace the plan of God and watch for moments that become fond memories of a buffalo better than you could have ever imagined. It's all in your perspective.

Like I have said, some buffaloes are not always a great experience, as we discovered in Chapter Two. Some are surprises for sure and tend to land on the low side. So what do you do with a buffalo that is less than desirable?

Was there anything joyful about what we experienced through COVID? Or maybe there is something other than the pandemic touching your life. No matter where you find yourself, there are days you'll need to choose and find joy in your circumstances. It is what you and I do in these circumstances that determine our attitude and the direction we take.

In Acts 13, Paul and Barnabas set out on their first missionary journey preaching the good news of Jesus Christ. Many believed the Way, but when the Jews saw the popularity of Paul's message, they became jealous and drove them out of their district. Paul and Barnabas shook off the dust of their feet and moved on. And this is what's said of them: "They were continually filled with joy and the Holy Spirit" (Acts 13:52).

Really? Filled with joy? How did they find joy in their journey when they were being persecuted? How do you and I find joy in our journeys when faced with less than desirable circumstances? It's a choice! A daily choice only you can choose.

Here are three steps to experience joy during difficult times:

1. Embrace the test.

> *Consider it all joy, my brethren, when you*
> *encounter various trials, knowing that the*
> *testing of your faith produces endurance.*

(James 1:2-3)

The meaning behind the word "testing" is compared to a silversmith's process when refining silver. The silversmith first heats up the silver until the impurities—the unclean and unwanted substances—rise to the top. From there, he scoops them away and repeats the process until he sees his reflection in the silver. Then, he knew the refining process was complete. This is the similar process God uses with us. God is the Silversmith and we are the silver. He continues to refine us until He sees His reflection in us. So, embrace the testing you are experiencing, and remember that God knows the end result of what it will take to make you more like Him. Oh, that you would come out of this time refined with a stronger faith, a purer heart, and a better representation of Christ.

2. Remember that your life is hidden with Christ in God

> *Therefore, if you have been raised up with*
> *Christ, keep seeking the things above, where*
> *Christ is, seated at the right hand of God. Set*
> *your mind on the things above, not on the*
> *things that are on earth. For you have died and*
> *your life is hidden with Christ in God.*
> (Colossians 3:1-3)

God's desire is for us to experience a total oneness with Him. In Jeremiah 45:5, Jeremiah essentially told Baruch, his scribe, "Don't seek great things for yourself. God has given you the best gift you could ask for—Your life." Yes, your life is a gift! Treasure it. You are chosen, blessed, blameless, and redeemed. Because your precious life in hidden with Christ, you're able to have a deep sense of acceptance from your heavenly Father that surpasses the extent of the world's acceptance, which in turn produces the joy only experienced from an intimate relationship with Jesus.

3. Watch for small opportunities to express gratitude.

> *Whatever you do in word or deed,*
> *do all in the name of the Lord Jesus,*
> *giving thanks through Him*
>
> *to God the Father.*
>
> (Colossians 3:17)

Gratitude is a word used to express thankfulness and praise. A general attitude of thanksgiving in both the trials and blessings of life characterizes the Christian. The apostle Paul exhorts us in Scripture to give thanks for all things, in all circumstances (Ephesians 5:20; 1 Thessalonians 5:18), even in suffering (James 1:1-4).

- Choose to experience the blessing of gratitude.
- Choose to find beauty in small moments of joy.
- Choose to live life in the present and not the future.
- Choose today to make a difference in someone's day.

Each day is a gift.

So teach us to number our days,
that we may present to You a heart of wisdom.
(Psalm 90:12)

As I am writing this chapter, I've had time to reflect on some of my buffaloes over fifty-seven years. Most have been incredible highs, while some at first glance could represent lows. But with a deeper dive into my memory and hindsight, they became some of the greatest training grounds in my life:

- While becoming an adult, I realized just how precious my childhood was.

- Marrying my high school sweetheart brought many buffalo moments that brought much laughter and its own dose of tears, too. Yet growth abounded.

- Walking through a life-threatening disease was no walk in the park, but the buffaloes that came along the way were life-changing and gave me many opportunities to see God move in ways I would have never experienced and develop a more intimate relationship with my Savior.

- Watching God move through a ministry He called me to many years before He birthed it gave me a front-row seat to a miracle in the making. Yes, in the making—lessons learned in the waiting. In your waiting time, you will come to know God in a deeper way. Desire to be the best learner you can be by seeking Him with all your heart and trusting Him to complete what He began.

- Raising two girls, who have become my very best friends, is a delight.

Although I must say, the greatest buffalo has been becoming a Mimi. Never did I think my heart could expand and explode in the ways it has. Yes, raising both my girls was a high (with a few lows thrown in over the years, ha-ha). But getting a second chance at parenting has been a delight. Of course, I am not the main caregiver but a contributor. Talk about perspective. When you get a ''redo,'' you see things from a totally different angle. Grand-parenting has been such a joy, and I wouldn't exchange it for the world. And it's so fun being able to provide one buffalo after another in their lives—even if they receive one too many stuffed animals!

Oh, and the wonder of it all! The wonder has been such a buffalo. Wondering what God would do on the other side of the experience builds your faith, anticipation, and trust in His sovereign plan. It's in the in-between time when God catches our true allegiance.

We know in our minds God is trustworthy, but do we allow that truth to penetrate our hearts in order to walk it out through our days? Trust is a choice! It is a choice we make every day. Some days it is harder than others, and we become discouraged and downtrodden. But in the end we need to, "trust in the Lord with all [our] heart and not lean on [our] own understanding. In all [our] ways acknowledge Him, and He will make [our] paths straight" (Proverbs 3:5-6).

Will you trust Him with your tomorrow? Will you trust Him even when . . .? Will you trust Him to write the second part of your story?

To truly understand why God will do what He says, we must fully understand His character and the attributes that prove He is trustworthy.

1. He is **truthful** (John 17:17). Since truth is the very essence of His nature, it's impossible for Him to lie. Therefore, we can believe in His promises because

He always tells the truth. He is trustworthy even when others aren't.

2. He is **good** (Psalm 119:68). His character is good, pure, and right. He desires for us to follow Him with our whole heart, mind, and soul. When we veer off course, He lovingly disciplines us for our good, which, in turn, leads us back on track.

3. He is **love** (1 John 4:19). He loved us before we loved Him. His promises are always based on our best interests.

4. He is **for us** (Psalm 56:9b). The cross is the ultimate proof of His love for you and me. Jesus died for our sins. If He loved us enough to show the ultimate act of love (laying down one's life), we have no reason to doubt Him, His Word, or His plans. Fix your eyes on Him.

So whenever you find yourself discouraged, doubtful, or fearful, remind yourself of the character of God. As His children, we have an amazing heavenly Father who is for us. Who, then, can be against us (Romans 8:31)?

He can do far more, above and beyond all that you ask or think. To Him be the glory.

There is so much to learn while you wait and trust Him with the next step. It's your choice to trust. Will you trust Him with the next step? Will you trust Him to teach you along the way?

- A season of difficulty can bring growth.
- A season of weeping can bring healing.
- A season of loss can bring gratitude.
- A season of silence can bring depth.
- A season of joy can bring blessings.
- A season of love can bring respect.
- A season of wait can bring great anticipation.

It's all in your perspective.

Colossians 3:15-17 gives us three powerful steps that will help change our perspective and increase our gratitude: First, we must allow the peace of Christ to rule in our hearts. Second, we should display thankfulness. And finally, we have to let His Word richly dwell in us.

> *And let the peace of Christ* rule in your hearts,
> *to which indeed you were called in one body.*
> *And* be thankful. *Let* the word of Christ richly
> dwell in you, *teaching and admonishing one*
> *another in all wisdom, singing psalms and*
> *hymns and spiritual songs, with thankfulness*
> *in your hearts to God. And whatever you*
> *do, in word or deed, do everything in the*
> *name of the Lord Jesus, giving thanks*
> *to God the Father through Him.*
>
> (emphasis author)

Incorporating these steps will help you embrace your buffaloes and allow Jesus to get involved in the intimate details of your life. He can give you an amazing surprise! You can rest assured that there is nothing you're going through God doesn't see, know, and understand.

Similarly, your attitude can be a game changer in your day, too. Oh, not just in your day, but for all those around you. Remember, there is only one thing you can control in your life, and that is your attitude. No matter what you experienced yesterday, you have the option to change your attitude for today! Some days, we just need a purposeful attitude adjustment. No matter if it's in the home, workplace, the grocery store, or enjoying coffee with a group of friends, your attitude can set the stage for others.

Wouldn't it be fun to be someone else's buffalo? You heard me correctly. You could be someone's buffalo: a sweet word of encouragement, a surprise visit, a return of another's cart at the grocery store, a flower on your co-worker's desk . . . it will most likely be a deliberate act on your part, but an unexpected blessing on the receiver's part.

So, what do you say? Will you have a fresh perspective while watching for your buffaloes?

Reflection Questions

1. Is discovering your daily buffalo a new concept? If yes, will you add it to your end of day's reflection?

2. From the list of God's trustworthiness, what spoke to you?

3. What powerful step from Colossians 3:15-17 do you have to incorporate into your day that will help give you a better outlook: allow the peace of Christ to rule in your hearts, display thankfulness, or let His Word richly dwell in you?

4. What can you do to be someone else's buffalo?

Four
Perspective is Everything

You have heard it said a million times (okay, maybe not a million times, but a lot), perspective is everything. Change your perspective, and you may be able to change your life.

I remember the day I walked the aisle to accept Jesus Christ as my Savior. I was only eighteen years old and unsure of what my future held. I hardly recall the message preached, but what I do remember is the Word spoken was meant especially for me. (You know what I am talking about, right? It's a time when it feels like there is no one else in the room but you and God.) Nothing else mattered except the very moment in which I was living. That very hot 1983 summer night in a church without air conditioning, God changed my life forever . . . which meant He changed my perspective and direction. The life-changing event didn't shift everything at once, but it did give me fresh eyes to see the world, my situation, and life differently. And for the next thirty-nine years, God would still be adjusting my thinking.

This is what I know: in the unknown I meet God every single time, while trying to keep my eyes focused on Him and not the situation. Doing this helps me see a circumstance from God's perspective and not my own outlook.

If you've never experienced the love of God I have shared about, there's no time like the present. You can accept Jesus into your heart and allow Him to change your life in the stillness of your room right now. All you need to do is ask Jesus to become the high of your day by understanding that as the living expression of God, He has reconciled you in His fleshly body through death on the cross in order to present you before the Father holy, blameless, and beyond reproach (Colossians 1:19-22). You now are welcomed into eternal glory because of John 3:16: "For God so loved the world, that He gave His only begotten Son, that whoever believes in Him shall not perish, but have eternal life."

Loving Jesus and allowing Him to dictate my days doesn't make me any less human. I still feel hurts and uncertainties, and I have a skewed vision from time to time. I battle to maintain a good perspective just like the rest of us, but I continually try to refocus the lenses through which I look. When we allow Jesus to be at the center of our day, we will see things more from a heavenly perspective than an earthly one. A little deeper dive into Colossians 3:1-4 will help set our minds on things above rather than focus on the here and now.

Therefore, if you have been raised with Christ,
keep seeking the things that are above, where
Christ is, seated at the right hand of God. Set
your minds on the things that are above,
not on the things that are on earth. For
you have died, and your life is hidden with
Christ in God. When Christ, who is our life,
is revealed, then you also will be revealed
with Him in glory.

(emphasis author)

Setting our minds on things above does not mean that we should live in a mystical fog or neglect our affairs in the here and now. What it does mean is that we are not only to be concerned with the trivialities of the temporal, but we should also view everything (actions and relationships) against the backdrop of eternity. With this new perspective on life, the eternal will surely have an impact on the temporal.[1] When we have eternal love on our minds and hearts, it is easier to love others as God has commanded us to love (John 13:34).

Keep in mind, we can only have this perspective because we are hidden in Christ with God (Colossians 3:3). The union that exists between Christ and His people is hidden from the eyes of the men and women of this world. Though they see us going about our daily tasks, they are unaware that our strength, by which we live and move and have our being, is drawn from God. That is why it is so important to reach up to God daily for our strength—so that we will be able to act justly, love mercy, and walk humbly with our God (Micah 6:8).

A lot of times, our perspective is directly correlated to our thoughts and position before God. Our eyes are the pathway to our being. If they are good, we will see God clearly. But if our eyes are evil, they will shut out the light, clouding our view of God. A "pure" eye is one that is fixed on God. Matthew 6:22-23 clearly states the parallel, "The eye is the lamp of the body; so then if your eye is clear, your whole body will be full of light. But if your eye is bad, your whole body will be full of darkness. If then the light that is in you is darkness, how great is the darkness!"

Keeping your eyes from evil will help you to see more clearly. Right thinking will impact your actions and motivate you to live wisely. Where you position God is how He will relate to you. John 14:21 tells us, "The one who has My commandments and keeps them is the one who loves Me; and the one who loves Me will be loved by My Father, and I will love him and will reveal Myself to him." Jesus will disclose Himself to those who seek Him, love Him, and desire to keep His commandments.

Proverbs 23:7 says, "For as he thinks within himself, so he is." What you and I think will dictate our actions. What you dwell on will be a plumb line for processing a situation.

Too many times our perspective is altered by what we think we should do, who we should be, and how we should act. The *should* mindset most times will lead to disappointment. Avoiding this perception will lead to a happier lifestyle— not a perfect lifestyle, but one grounded in the truths of who you are in Christ.

Changing your inner self-talk can transform the way you carry yourself and feel about yourself, as well as give you a different view for the world around you. If you replace negative talk with positive truth, God will guard your heart and mind with what He thinks about you. First Peter 2:9 says, "But you are a chosen race, a royal priesthood, a holy nation, a people for *God's* own possession, so that you may proclaim the excellencies of Him who has called you out of darkness into His marvelous light." Right thinking begins with the words you speak to yourself and where your thoughts are fixed—on what is true, honorable, right, pure, lovely, admirable, excellent, and worthy of praise. It's time to stop the cycle of wrong thinking; instead, start dwelling on the truths of God and allow His promise of peace to wash over your mind.

I can remember a time in my life, after coming to a saving knowledge of Jesus Christ, when I was not walking in the light of God. One morning while I was driving, it felt like my spiritual eyes were replaced with worldly eyes. I don't know exactly how to explain it, except that my worldview took on a whole new vision—one not worthy of my calling. I was stunned by the experience and realized I was out of the will of God. Something had to change. God didn't move. I did.

Have you ever found yourself in the same situation? If so, return to God. He will receive you with open arms. He desires for you to have a pure heart, clean hands, and clear eyes so that your whole body will be full of light and have no darkness in it at all. How fixed on God are you? How in tune are you with God's ways?

Freedom comes when you and I commit to God, resist the devil, draw near to God, and purify our hearts in the presence of the Lord. "Submit," "resist," "draw near," and "purify" are active verbs that make a difference in defending our hearts against Satan's attack on our lives. James 4:7-10 gives us this remedy for a renewed focus:

> *Submit therefore to God. Resist the devil*
> *and he will flee from you. Draw near to God*
> *and He will draw near to you. Cleanse your*
> *hands, you sinners; and purify your hearts,*
> *you double-minded. Be miserable and mourn*
> *and weep; let your laughter be turned into*
> *mourning and your joy to gloom. Humble*
> *yourselves in the presence of the Lord,*
> *and He will exalt you.*

If you continually refresh your mind with the following steps, you will be more likely to have a fresh perspective: 1) commit your ways to God; 2) come close to Him; 3) cleanse; and 4) confess. My pastor once put it like this: *Give In, Get Close, Clean Up, and Get Down.*

Humbling yourself before God will allow Him to have lordship over your life. Because He is all-supreme, God wants to be the main authority in your life and the master designer of your days. Keep Jesus as the Source of truth— your true north. As you fix your eyes on Jesus, the author and perfecter of your faith (Hebrews 12:2), and abandon yourself to depths of intimacy with Him, you will discover the freedom that only He can supply. Ask God to, "open [your] eyes, that [you] may behold wonderful things from [His] law" (Psalm 119:18).

By gazing upon His goodness and strength, you will hold the might to resist all that is displeasing to God. For what you believe deep in your soul will be what you live out. Your internal convictions will dictate your outward actions.

By denying Satan the attention he longs for, he will eventually give up. Yes, this resistance to sin will require a mindset shift and strength, but peace will flood your soul with each decision to seek God and clothe yourself in His righteousness. Again, this statement applies: obedience is up to you, but the outcome is up to God.

Satan's goal is to make life a living hell for believers. That is why you must daily renew your mind: "Therefore let us lay aside the deeds of darkness and put on the armor of light. Let us behave properly as in the day, not in carousing and drunkenness, not in sexual promiscuity and sensuality, not in strife and jealousy. But put on the Lord Jesus Christ, and make no provision for the flesh in regard to its lusts" (Romans 13:12-14). The promise of Satan fleeing from you will require an active pursuit of surrender to God. Stand up to the Devil and resist him, and he will turn and run away from the Jesus who lives in you.

Yes, you will experience the freedom that Christ came to provide for you through His death on the cross and give you eyes to see more clearly. He is the One who is able to protect you from stumbling, and to make you stand in the presence of His glory, blameless with great joy (Jude 1:24).

As you stand in His presence with confidence and a clear conscience, you will be able to have open eyes and a sharper perspective toward those around you. John 4:35 (NIV) says, 'I tell you, open your eyes and look at the fields! They are ripe for harvest."

We are not meant for isolation but for relationship. Will you ask God to open your eyes to the needs of those around you and make you available for ministry opportunities? There is no time like the present to be watchful. The importance for today is—now.

He is calling you and me to open our eyes. Won't you ask Him to anoint your eyes to see beyond what you can naturally perceive? We should respond in faith like Joshua and Caleb did in Numbers 13. They were not dismayed by the giants in the land like their cohorts, who were intimidated by the people that possessed the land they had scouted. Rather, Joshua and Caleb saw the positive. Their perspective was very different from the other spies because they viewed the situation through a set of positive lenses. Will your response be the same as Joshua and Caleb's declaration, "We must go up and take possession of the land because we can certainly conquer it!" (Numbers 13:30 HCSB)? Will you say yes to what God is asking of you during this season of your life? If you pay close attention, you will see God at work all around you and discover ministry opportunities right before you . . . . All you need to do is open your eyes. Luke 12:35 tells us, "Be dressed in readiness, and keep your lamp lit." We are supposed to be ready and actively waiting for Christ's return, which involves being watchful regarding the needs around us and living in a state of eagerness when the Lord returns. Am I dressed in readiness? Are you dressed in readiness? Do we keep our light lit? In the Greek, "readiness" means "to gird one's self; to equip one's self with knowledge of the truth; be prepared."[2]

If we would be adequately prepared for action, we must value time in God's presence as supreme over being bombarded by the world's influences. We must build our lives on a Person, the Lord Jesus Christ. Preparation is essential to Christian living. The greatest way we can prepare ourselves for the days ahead is to be found in Him through the reading of His Word. His Word will equip us to handle and respond to trials, temptations, adversities, and successes that undoubtedly will come our way.

What does it look like to dress ourselves for readiness?

- First, we must meet with God in the stillness of His presence and apply Colossians 3:12-15 (NLT) to our daily routine: ". . . clothe ourselves with tenderhearted mercy, kindness, humility, gentleness, and patience. Make allowances for each other's faults, and forgive anyone who offends you. Remember, the Lord forgave you, so you must forgive others. Above all, clothe yourselves with love, which binds us all together in perfect harmony. And let the peace that comes from Christ rule in your hearts. For as members of one body you are called to live in peace. And always be thankful."

- Second, we should hide God's Word in our hearts so we will have an answer for others, as Second Timothy 4:2 tells us: 'Preach the word; be ready in season and out of season; [correct], rebuke, and exhort, with great patience and instruction."

- Finally, but the most important, we should keep preparing for Christ's return and practice righteousness. First Peter 1:15-16 says, "But like the Holy One who called you, be holy yourselves also in all your behavior; because it is written, 'You shall be holy, for I am holy.'"'

Reading and memorizing His Word will be a guard and protection that will sustain you and keep you. And continue to dress yourself with the righteousness of God so that you will be found ready at His return.

What does your wardrobe consist of? Does it only consist of an exterior adornment, or is it an internal sacrifice yielding to the Spirit of God, who causes you to follow Him closer and glorify Him with each passing day? Oh, that you and I would be women who dress ourselves with strength and make our arms strong (Proverbs 31:17) and wear the belt of truth (Ephesians 6:14) to secure our foundation so that we will be ready for the days ahead, knowing that we have a God who goes before us.

As I reflect on the past thirteen years of ministry and the leap I took to follow His call, I am overwhelmed with all God has placed in my heart—what He has done, provided, and completed. My biggest prayer was that I wouldn't move ahead if God didn't go before me. It has been far more above and beyond all that I could have imagined (Ephesians 3:20). When I took the initial step to move out with God in 2010, I knew God had called me into full-time ministry. Yes, I fearfully took the leap with excitement and great anticipation, although at times the only way to do something was to do it while afraid.

Relying on God will always be the pathway to knowing it is not all about you, but all about what *God* can do. However, this doesn't mean you sit on the sidelines and be the best cheerleader you can be. No, it means you get in the game with the talents and gifts God has given you and allow Him to develop them along the way so that you can be ready. Just as Joshua and the priests had to put their feet into the water to cross the Jordan (Joshua 3:13), I had to take that step of faith and trust God with the outcome. And the same is true for you. Open your spiritual eyes to all that surrounds you!

Has God placed a dream or desire in your heart? Once He gives you the green light to go after those dreams, you must make a move. A pursuit of excellence is what will distinguish you from someone else who goes after it half-heartedly. Go after your dream with an 'I-will-finish-this-task" mentality. Is today the day you take that risk? If you don't take the risk, it may be the one thing you regret at the end of your life. If God is asking you to go after your dream with an 'I-will-finish-this-task" mentality, how are you performing the task? Have you fallen short of aiming high? If yes, what will it take for you to refocus?

Even if fear has struck you, don't allow it to paralyze you. First Corinthians 2:1-5 was an encouragement to me during one of my early morning readings, where Paul said,

> *And when I came to you, brothers and* sisters,
> *I did not come as* someone *superior in speaking*
> *ability or wisdom, as I proclaimed to you the*
> *testimony of God. For I determined to know*
> *nothing among you except Jesus Christ, and Him*
> *crucified. I also was with you in weakness and*
> *fear, and in great trembling, and my message*
> *and my preaching were not in persuasive words*
> *of wisdom, but in demonstration of the Spirit*
> *and of power, so that your faith would not rest*
> *on the wisdom of mankind, but on the power of*
> *God.*

Even after a previous discouraging experience (Acts 17), Paul still went to Corinth. Disappointment didn't stop him from doing what God had called him to do. Although he accepted his next assignment with weakness, fear, and trembling, he still moved ahead. If Paul can fearfully walk into his next mission, so can you. Remind yourself that God goes before you and will make a way where there seems to be no way. Knowing He is on the other side of your uncertainty allows God to show His power, not your own strength.

What change in perspective is God asking you to consider?

- Reset your day?
- Rethink your commitments?
- Refocus your thoughts?
- Review your planner?
- Reassess your goals?
- Reevaluate your relationships?
- Revise your time?

Once you have examined the areas for which you may need to have a different mindset, what will you do to make the shift in your thinking? Remember, it may take time to make the switch, but every step taken in the right direction will be worth the effort. Never stop reassessing your life because it's what will keep you both spiritually sharp and completely reliant on God. Having an eternal perspective will help keep all things in balance and focused on what's important.

Reflection Questions

1. Have you experienced the love of God and accepted Jesus as your Savior? If yes, how has it changed your perspective? If you still need to, will today be the day of your salvation?

2. Do you have a should mindset?

3. Has God opened your eyes to the needs of those around you? What is He asking you to do?

4. Has God placed a dream or desire in your heart? What will you do to move forward with that dream?

Five
Silver-Lining Faith

In the midst of the pandemic, most of us hesitated to keep our medical check-ups, dentist's visits, eye exams, and other important appointments. Well, at least I did, due to the uncertain risk of being near others. I had to work very hard to make them happen. During the pandemic, I had my yearly cardiology appointment, and to my delight, I found the silver lining amidst yet another visit. The common expression "every cloud has a *silver lining*" can mean that even in a low event or situation, we can find a buffalo that causes us to have a positive reaction. We use the expression to say that no matter how bad something appears at the moment, there will be something better around the corner.

It wasn't the first time the words of a nurse comforted and encouraged me. Through many hospital stays over the years, I don't believe I would've survived without the wisdom and care of the many nurses God placed in my life. And this divine meeting was no different. We began the initial conversation like any other appointment: "How are you, and what brings you in today?" After some small talk, we began to discuss what *normal* in our day looked like. Here was the silver lining—her perspective was extremely refreshing although she had no idea how her words would fall like fresh morning dew on my ears. Her response was not the common reply of loss, disunity, or distress that surrounded us. It was an attitude of "Let's move forward the best we can and be careful doing it." What a great perspective—to embrace change instead of being caught up in what once was. Staying put and refusing to move forward will deter us from experiencing the hope to which God calls us.

While reading through the Book of Job, verse 10 of chapter 2 questioned my perspective and brought the sentiment of this unnamed nurse's attitude to light in my early morning devotion: "'Should we only accept the good things from the hand of God and never anything bad?'" Wow! As I look back over my life and even the pandemic year, what I have learned is what the world deems as bad, God uses it for the good in terms of our spiritual growth. God's Word encourages us to keep our gaze on Jesus, remaining in His steadfast love:

- In the darkness of our days He reveals who He is and whose we are (Isaiah 45:3).
- He shines His light on our path (Psalm 119:105).
- He gives His strength if we accept our weakness (2 Corinthians 12:9-11).
- He softens a humble heart (Ezekiel 36:26).

- He gives fresh eyes to those who fix their gaze on Him (Hebrews 12:2).
- He increases wisdom to those who ask for wiser days (James 1:5).
- He gives more of the Holy Spirit to those who ask for it (Luke 11:13).

There are things you and I will never learn without having a broken spirit or going to a hard place with God. He wants to be your dayspring. He wants to be the silver-lining breakthrough in your dark, long days. There is always something good to be found if you look hard and long enough and don't lose faith. So if you're experiencing hardship, tough days, or a tired spirit, look to Him for renewal and know He is for you and walks beside you. His mercies are new every single day! Oh, that you and I would not be like Lot's wife, looking back to what we once had (Genesis 19:26), but holding fast to the promise of what lies ahead, walking in the light of His goodness and grace.

As I look back even further than the pandemic to another time and season, the counselor I mentioned in Chapter One spoke encouragement into my life during the height of my illness, and ultimately I saw the silver lining from that very low period of my life. God had a bigger plan for using my life—one that would bring hope to women.

I know you may find it hard to embrace some of your experiences as God's plan. However, in every place a purpose exists, and it's up to you to experience this purpose to its fullest. Once you are able to view your life as a plan from God, you will begin to walk in His ways rather than walking in the light of your own understanding. He has a plan and it's so much greater than we could humanly understand. Keep your eyes focused on Him and He will illumine your path and give you eyes to see beyond your own understanding.

I am sure as you look in the rear view mirror, hindsight is 20/20. Hindsight is a gift because you learn from what has happened in the past, gain an understanding for the future, and develop better skills to share with those you lead. At times, though, you can become stuck in the past, looking at either failures or successes. Yes, draw wisdom from all the experiences to move forward with better insight; however, you may need to refocus on where God is taking you in the future. Søren Kierkegaard, a Danish philosopher, theologian, poet, social critic, and religious author, said it best when he wrote, "Life can be understood backwards, but it must be lived forward."

Proverbs 4:25-27, as rendered by The Passion Translation (TPT), will help give you the vision to keep moving forward despite battling setbacks:

> *Set your gaze on the path before you. With*
> *fixed purpose, looking straight ahead, ignore*
> *life's distractions. Watch where you're*

*going! Stick to the path of truth, and
the road will be safe and smooth before
you. Don't allow yourself to be sidetracked
for even a moment or take the detour that
leads to darkness.*

Yes, keep your focus on Jesus! Move out with passion to what He has set before you and work at it with all your heart.

There are times like my nurse story at the beginning of this chapter when you recognize the silver lining almost automatically, and then there are other times like the counselor story when it may take decades for you to lift your head enough to notice the silver lining. But just like declaring what your daily buffalo is, you will need to be watchful for the silver lining. Be deliberate in shifting your perspective to have a positive attitude.

Asaph, while writing Psalm 73, wondered why the wicked prosper. Focusing on the actions of others, he started to take his eyes off God until one day when he went into the sanctuary of God (Psalm 73:17). This sanctuary place can be described as a consecrated thing, a holy place, a cleansing river, or the secret place. When Asaph entered this sanctuary, God revealed his heart to him and changed his perspective from a heart of bitterness to a life of gratitude.

In the same way, when we meet with God, He can change the way we view situations and in turn help us discover a silver lining. Sometimes it is our own heart that needs cauterizing. This is exactly what happened to Asaph when he realized he was becoming bitter (Psalm 73:21). But then He began to remember God's sovereignty and refocused his thoughts on his own life rather than becoming caught up with the actions of the wicked. In conclusion, Asaph knew the nearness of God was his good. Therefore, he refocused, making God his refuge so that he could share all of God's works (Psalm 73:28).

If you find yourself a little like Asaph, wondering where God is in all of life, or your thoughts are centered on the ways of others, return to the Lord and seek Him that you may live (Amos 5:6). We know that God searches for those of us who fully commit our hearts to Him (2 Chronicles 16:9). Enter into this secret place with God and experience His security. Seek Him with all your heart and ask Him to become greater in your life so that He will reveal His purpose and bring clarity to a situation. At times it's as simple as meeting with God, being quiet long enough to hear His still, small voice, which will change your perspective and help you see through all the chaos that clouds your view. (Okay, it may not be simple, but it's necessary.)

I clearly remember a year when my girls were in elementary school. It was a time when my days felt like they were spinning out of control because the to-do list exceeded the allotted twenty-four hours. Between the Christian school they attended, a neighborhood Bible study held in my home, a children's program I oversaw at our church, a newly formed community Bible study I organized, plus managing our home, something had to give. And give, it did. My relationship with the Lord, that is.

You see, I was doing all these good things for God, but I was missing the most important part of my day—time with Him. Oh, I would walk by the chair that once occupied my early morning moments and whisper to God, "I'll be there when..."

Sometimes, you can allow the clutter in your life to overshadow the necessity of living close to God. When you allow your heart, mind, and soul to be captivated by your time with God, He will reveal the most important next step in your hour, day, month, and task and give you a clearer vision. Let His presence bring order to your thoughts as you set aside alone time with the One who holds your days. Allow His peace to permeate a few moments of your day to bring wisdom, clarity, and direction. The nearness of God is as close as you make it. You make time for what is important, don't you?

Many of us have bought into the cultural lie that a busy life is a productive one. As women, we thrive on productivity, but it cannot be at the expense of our alone time with God. I am all for a balanced life, which is what we, twenty-first-century women, try to achieve in so many areas of our lives, but the one area that should be unbalanced is your time with God. This should be the one thing that tips the teeter-totter to the one side, over all the others.

And that same chair that should have been occupying my morning can be the same one you avoided because you shy away from meeting with God—for you know He may reveal areas of your own life that need to be addressed, just like Asaph's embittered heart. I encourage you to not run from God but sprint toward Him. Even though there may be hard things to hear from Him, His words are always ones that bring growth and direction, and they are also life-giving and life-changing if we allow them to penetrate our hearts.

Reflection Questions

1. Share a time you discovered the silver lining of a less than desirable time or situation.

2. Have you ever become so busy doing the work of the Lord that your relationship with Him took a toll? What change needed to take place?

3. Have you established a sanctuary
   place with God? Is it a priority in your
   day to meet with Him there?

Six
Moments
Matter

While reading Isaiah 40:28-31, the Lord put the name of a friend on my heart. I felt the need to text her these encouraging words: *"The everlasting God, the creator of the ends of the earth, does not become weary or tire."* But then, the battle in my mind began. My thoughts went back and forth like a game of ping-pong . . . to send the text *or* not to send. I thought to myself, *Did I hear God correctly?*

So, with slight hesitation, I sent the text. God knew how His words would land on her heart. All He was asking from me was obedience. Soon after I hit "send," I received a beautiful text back from her. Then days later, she called me to share God's hug to her through that text. This reminded me to be faithful and obedient in each moment. Moments do count. Small moments and big moments are important, and you and I are supposed to be faithful in both. Yesterday is gone, tomorrow is uncertain. Today is here—use it wisely.

Do you remember the quote in Chapter One from Mark Batterson, "Time is measured in minutes; life is measured in moments"? It's during those ordinary moments when you catch a glance from your child that melts your heart, an unexpected hand was held, a call brings a smile after a long day, a text received boosts your day, or a kind gesture encourages you to keep on keeping on. It's not always the great big events that mark our days but the small moments that link them together. That one "little" text, for example, changed the attitude of my friend receiving it.

Psalm 90:12 (NASB) tells us "to number our days, that we may present to You a heart of wisdom." Other versions say,

- "So teach us to consider our mortality, so that we might live wisely" (NET).
- "Oh! Teach us to live well! Teach us to live wisely and well" (MSG)!
- "Teach us to realize the brevity of life, so that we may grow in wisdom" (NLT).

The plea to number our days, live wisely, and realize the brevity of life is a request to comprehend how short our lives are in light of God's eternal nature. Yes, we must consider God's ownership over our lives. God is eternal, and our lives are a vapor—quickly passing (James 4:14).

It seems as soon as we create a special moment, it becomes a memory. This is the very reason it's important to be present in the moment and soak up as much as we can like there's no tomorrow. I have a drawer filled with many photos from years gone by, a few creative memory albums under the coffee table, plenty of the old-fashioned style albums (you know, the ones in which you slide the pictures into a sleeve and write the memory next to the photo), and unprinted photos on my computer and smartphone.

Both our girls are married with children of their own. After they had their sons, they both wanted to look through their albums to see if there were resemblances of themselves in their boys. As our girls were growing up, I wanted to try to capture the important stages of their lives by keeping a special box with their accomplishments.

Certificates.

Written letters.

Drawn pictures.

Papier-mâché animals.

And so much more.

When reopening the overstuffed boxes, we laugh and remember,

The whens.

The what ifs.

The joys.

My husband's dad had some of their family's old videos converted to DVDs. We have had so much fun at our gatherings watching the aunts and uncles in their prime of life, in high school, and at younger ages. Watching all our nieces and nephews laughing and seeing their parents' resemblances to themselves brings smiles to our hearts. We are so thankful that Dad captured those precious moments. And the next generation is—well, I guess you can say—blessed.

Sometimes there are blushing faces, but for the most part, pure laughter and joy. There are many different ways we can relive our lives that are vital in recalling the memories. Some will bring a tear to our eyes, others laughter. Hopefully, each memory captured will point us to delight in seeing where we once were and from where we have come. They may have their own style, but they all have the same purpose—making memories.

As I grow older, I try so hard to keep the memories alive. But as hard as I try, there are ones that slip by me. I have even looked at a picture of one of our girls when they were small and wondered, *Which girl is that?* I never thought I could forget, but I did. Some memories we wish we could forget, don't we? But all your memories are part of who you are and what you are becoming.

The enjoyable memories are so much easier to reflect upon. These are moments in the sun—ones we want to remember—our highlight reel. But then there are those that aren't as memorable. Or are they? Because these moments, if we allow them, can be the ones that change the trajectory of our days. The difficult memories are the ones in which I have learned the most about myself and the sovereignty of God.

Then there are preciously stored events in the memory boxes of our intellect—ones with no picture captured, just a vivid snapshot in our memory bank.

- A toddler's smile while swinging.
- A kindergartner's packed lunch box.
- A play date with friends at the community park.
- The joys of a sticker received from a memorized Bible verse.
- A middle-schooler's first dance.
- A high-schooler's search for independence.
- A college student's source of accomplishment and dreams of the future.
- A written letter from my daughter, now friend.
- A late-night conversation before a wedding day.
- The homecoming of each new grand-baby.

These are milestone moments, ones that will never be repeated but forever implanted into your psyche. Even though some of your photos are hard to look at and you may not want to recapture specific events, it is always good to have that rear-view mirror glimpse. Captured moments along the way help you remember the road you have traveled and all that God has brought you through to appreciate the present journey of life. They will be teachable moments, not for yourselves only, but also for those into which you want to impart memories of God's grace and love.

Abraham Lincoln said, "In the end, it's not the years in your life that count, it's the life in your years." In other words, it's not so much the days you have, but it is what we do with the days you are given. How might your life look different if you held this truth in your heart? What if you chose to live as though this was your last breath? Would you,

- Love more deeply?
- Forgive more promptly?
- Give more generously?
- Speak more graciously?
- Care more thoughtfully?
- Laugh more joyfully?
- Prioritize more carefully?

Let us not allow the spirit of idleness to win out. This view forgets that God has indeed saved us for good works (Ephesians 2:10), and that our lives and actions have meaning and purpose. Yes, moments count. Being intentional will take work on your part, but at the end of your day, you will be glad you went the extra mile. Each day let us be grateful, extend kindness, and have mercy on others.

How easy is it for us to become lost in the pursuit of money and success, chasing down the next win in the world's eyes, when God tells us in Joshua 1:8 what true success really is: "This Book of the Law shall not depart from your mouth, but you shall meditate on it day and night, so that you may be careful to do according to all that is written in it. For then you will make your way prosperous, and then you will have good success." Similarly, the psalmist in Psalm 1:2-3 (NASB) shares,

> *"But his delight is in the Law of the Lord,*
> *and on His Law he meditates day and night.*
> *He will be like a tree planted by streams of*
> *water, which yields its fruit in its season,*
> *and its leaf does not wither;*
> *and in whatever he does, he prospers."*

When we are consumed by His Word, we will be firmly rooted in Him and His ways.

Reading God's Word and passionately pursuing to live out what you read will bring success. Now, this is no promise that the blessed man won't ever fail. Yet even though failure is often part of his growth, he is the one who is led and guided by the indwelling Spirit. He is the one who maintains ongoing fellowship with the heavenly Father and presses on toward the high calling of Christ. This is true success.

We certainly can ask God to bless the works of our hands, just as Moses did in Psalm 90:17 (NET): "May our

Sovereign God extend His favor to us. Make our endeavors successful. Yes, make them successful."

This very verse became the stepping stone to launch the ministry God gave me years prior. I knew I couldn't do it without Him, and I didn't even want to try. This verse, instrumental before my personal ministry began, gave me the favor I needed when I helped start a community-wide Bible study in my hometown. I didn't want to take a step without His direction. Too many times I had tried to will my desires into existence. Don't misunderstand. We have to take the steps forward to what God's calling us to, but we can't make the move without His leading. As mentioned in a previous chapter, one thing we can control is our attitude.

Likewise, attitude's companion is effort. You control the amount of effort you set forth in the things God's calling you to pursue. Effort can set you apart from others who have a half-hearted approach. It is important to continue to strive for greatness and a strong pursuit of your dreams, even if it doesn't always work out.

Just as I needed Him in both the endeavors (which seemed monumental, and they were), I also still need Him in the everyday moments: taking the trip to the local market, planning the day's activities, walking with a friend, or adjusting my attitude after a poor response. Each deliberate step leads to my destiny ordained by God.

Let me close out this chapter with a story about a girl and her grandmother and making moments matter. When my grandmother, Jessie, turned ninety years old, I was asked to give a speech regarding her life. In front of fifty-plus people, I shared about her lasting legacy. It wasn't the money she would leave or the gifts she would distribute, but her love for family and her perseverance despite the deaths of two husbands, a daughter, two adult grandchildren and sons-in-law. It was her desire to live life to the fullest, which meant caring for those under her influence. She was always good at making you feel like you were the only one that mattered. Isn't that our desire—to make a mark on those who come behind us, a spiritual watermark that never fades away?

I once heard Chip Ingram, a well-known pastor, author, and teacher, say on his podcast, "Leave them something that money can't buy: Teach them to suffer well, and show them how to work unto the Lord, manage their finances, make wise decisions, and live grace-filled lives."

Now, that is an inheritance. We are not called just to leave something *to* those who come behind us, but to leave something *in* them. Our children and grandchildren are only entrusted to us for a short period of time. The legacy we will leave is the one we walk out every day.

A couple years after that monumental birthday, I received a call from my mother that my grandmother was gravely ill. I decided I needed to make a trip to her bedside in the nursing/rehabilitation home where she was living in Florida. All I can remember as I flew down was my prayer asking God to spare her life until I arrived. I wondered what I would say to her.

On my way to the nursing home, I stopped by a Christian bookstore and purchased a devotional by an author she was familiar with—Billy Graham. Upon my first visit with her, my mother and I went in together as she lay in her bed. We exchanged kisses, but I knew I could not stay long since it was late and I just wanted to be able to see her.

As I awakened the next morning with much emotion flooding my soul, I went for a daily visit by myself. When I arrived at the rehabilitation center, much to my surprise, she was at therapy. *Therapy*, I thought. *Wow, she is doing so much better.* It was an overnight miracle! The nurses were just as shocked as I was. They shared how there was such a difference in her after I arrived. My mother concurred, saying, "I think she was waiting for you to arrive. You gave her a reason to live."

As we shared stories with each other, I asked if I could read her the first devotional in her new book entitled, "Namesake." She agreed. I am named after my grandmother and have always felt honored by that. I don't remember all the details of the devotional—only that it asked what was behind a name. I was able to share about the honor I felt to carry her name ever since I was a little girl, along with the love I had for her. It was one of the sweetest moments of my life, one that I will cherish for a lifetime. But honestly, it was the words she shared with me that made the trip worth the blessing.

The Lord blessed her with nearly ninety-seven years, and our lives were rich from her years of love and commitment. One of the blessings for me was watching my daughters interact with their great-grandmother and watch them learn from her. And now that devotional I bought for her sits on my nightstand.

One custom I had while visiting my parents in Florida was to go for an early morning walk. After the walk ended, I would stop by my grandmother's house, which was in the same neighborhood as my parents', for my morning grapefruit from her tree, a Danish, and a cup of tea. As we would sit and converse, I would glean from her insight and years of wisdom. In the final year of my grandmother's life, our daughter carried on the custom I had started years earlier—an early-morning walk with a visit to her great-grandmother's home for breakfast. This was a legacy of love and devotion, as well as an inspiration and boost to an elderly woman to know that her life mattered.

It is important that if the Lord asks you to do something today, you make every effort to find the time. Hebrews 3:13-15 tells us,

> *But encourage one another day after day, as*
> *long as it is* still *called "Today," so that none*
> *of you will be hardened by the deceitfulness*
> *of sin. For we have become partakers of*
> *Christ, if we hold fast the beginning of our*
> *assurance firm until the end, while it is said,*
> *'Today if you hear His voice, do not harden*
> *your hearts, as when they provoked Me.'"*
>
> (emphasis author)

Today matters! Make the most of it, because what you build into those you influence will make a difference and leave a lasting impression on them, either good or bad. Again, we all have those moments we wish we could retract, but those are the ones from which we grow and learn. They are the moments you leave at the feet of Jesus, asking Him to forgive you, and then moving forward in God's power to live a lifestyle worthy of His calling. Let's make every moment count!

Reflection Questions

1. Do you struggle to live in the moment? If yes, how might you change your mindset to be present where you are and not look too far ahead?

2. How might your life look different if you had acted upon the truth of the saying, 'It's not so much the days we have, but it is what we do with the days we are given'?

3. Who is God asking you to encourage or speak life into their life? What will you do to make this a reality?

Seven
Living a
"Green Olive Tree" Life

How many of us are at our wit's end with the evil we see all around us? Guess what? Our times are not much different from the days of old—the days of the holy written Word of God. In Psalm 52, David confronts the wicked of his day (verses 1-5) and then shifts his focus to the Lord with a fresh perspective, stating his confidence in Him (verses 6-9). In verse 8, David stands firm in the assessment of his life when he says, "But as for me, I am like a green olive tree in the house of God; I trust in the faithfulness of God forever and ever." Can you and I declare the same thing about our lives, that we can live a "green olive tree" life—a life that flourishes no matter what trials, tribulations, or troubles we face? It's not about what the olive tree is as much as where it's located—"in the house of God." David was safe and secure in the midst of the wicked because he lived in the presence of God. You and I, like David, can stand above the wicked ways of our culture, too.

What does it mean to be like a green olive tree? When we are deemed a green olive tree, our desire is to be a peace-loving, alive, and fruitful person—flourishing and thriving. The olive tree and olive branch have been symbols of peace and reconciliation ever since the account of Noah's flood. When the dove brought Noah a plucked olive leaf in its beak, the olive branch represented new life sprouting on the earth (Genesis 8:11). The olive tree was alive and growing. The promise of the dove's olive branch was a new beginning for humanity, peace, and reconciliation with God that included renewal and revival. The slow and hearty growth of the olive tree also implies establishment and peace. Furthermore, the flowering olive tree is a symbol of beauty and abundance. The tree's fruitfulness and ability to thrive suggest the model of a righteous person.[1]

You and I can be women who display this style of living. Will it take a little elbow grease to live it out? Yes, it will. But it will be worth the effort. Here are four steps to living on purpose: a "Green Olive Tree" Life.

1. Live in the presence of God.

David declares, "But as for me, I am like a green olive tree in the house of God" (Psalm 52:8a). You and I, like this tree, should be rooted in the depths of God, where nourishment is found. The more you draw near to Him, the closer He will be to you (James 4:8). When we live in His presence, we will have a godlier perspective over a worldly viewpoint that will impact the way we live out our day.

2. Trust in the steadfast love of God.

David declares, "I trust in the steadfast love of God forever and ever" (Psalm 52:8b ESV). To trust in the Lord means that you have complete dependence and reliance on Him. He loved you before you loved Him (1 John 4:19). If He loved you enough to show the ultimate act of love (laying down one's life), you have no reason to doubt Him, His Word, or His plans for you. He is for you, not against you (Psalm 56:9).

3. Express thankfulness.

David testifies, "I will thank you forever, because you have done it" (Psalm 52:9a ESV). An attitude of thankfulness fosters a grateful heart. David's focus was on who did it, not what was done. This focus on the Lord enabled him to give thanks even through the trials. As we mature in the Lord, we will see difficult events as ones that strengthen us and prove our faith (1 Peter 1:7). "Rejoice always, pray without ceasing, in everything give thanks; for this is the will of God for you in Christ Jesus" (1 Thessalonians 5:16-18).

1. Wait on the Lord.

David announces, "I will wait for your name, for it is good, in the presence of the godly" (Psalm 52:9b). Lamentations 3:25 encourages us that, "the Lord is good to those who wait for Him, to the person who seeks Him." Although these verses bring hope, waiting is still difficult. But, as you embrace the waiting time, what you learn can be the catalyst of His future design. With a grateful heart, be thankful for all He teaches you in the waiting room, which will prepare you for each next step. In the waiting, He will clarify His purpose, develop patience, build anticipation, transform your character, and increase your intimacy with Him. As today unfolds, you may need to adjust your thinking, look straight ahead at Jesus, and let Him write your story. Release your expectations of what you envision happening and how you think it should unfold. Your days are in His hands, and He knows the best path in front of you. "For [you] are His workmanship, created in Him for good works, which He prepared beforehand that [you] would walk in them" (Ephesians 2:10).

Which of these steps will you need to embrace in this season of your life in order to live a "green olive tree" life—peaceful, flourishing, and thriving? If you skip one of these steps, your life can become out of rhythm with God's ways.

If that is where you find yourself, refocus your gaze on Him with a grateful heart and trust Him with the day in front of you.

Living a "green olive tree" life before others will help draw them to Jesus. It's not about living this life perfectly, but intentionally and in the present. Living a life secure, stable, and rooted in Christ will show a watching world where your strength comes from.

Yes, you can flourish in this life and enjoy blessings from God as you live out your days.

I have been blessed with knowing secure, influential, and right-living women in my life who have walked the path before me. As I think of them, I view them as women I respect and want to emulate. I say to them that they make growing older look attractive. They reply, "You have to grow older, but you don't have to grow old." It's all in the perspective you have.

Although these older saints may lose the vitality of their youth, they can still shine brightly. I love Proverbs 4:18 from the MSG version, "The ways of right-living people glow with light; the longer they live, the brighter they shine. But the road of wrongdoing gets darker and darker—travelers can't see a thing; they fall flat on their faces."

I would like to share with you about one of these women in my life. Meet Linda. She came into my life in 2001 through a conference I was helping to organize. Right from the first introduction, I knew she was someone I wanted to get to know better. Her confident demeanor and humble spirit drew me to the Jesus in her. She wasn't pretentious by any means, but secure in who she was. As the years passed from that first meeting, our interaction was sporadic—an event here and there, a lunch date to catch up, or an encouraging e-mail—until one day, when the Lord put her on my heart ten years later and I found myself across the table at a local restaurant sharing my heart, desires, and dreams with her. And since that day, she has been my "Elijah."

Elijah was a prophet and a miracle worker who lived in the northern kingdom of Israel during the reign of King Ahab. In First Kings 18, Elijah defended the worship of the Hebrew God over that of the Canaanite deity Baal. Elijah had a young pupil, Elisha, who became Elijah's successor after God took Elijah up in a whirlwind to heaven (2 Kings 2). For a season, Elijah was Elisha's guide and leader. Elijah displayed a secure strength of character to push forward despite every distraction, discouragement, and resistance.

Elisha followed and served his teacher until one day when they no longer walked together. I share this to say that depending on an "Elijah" in your life for the season God gives you this special relationship is such a blessing. And I am so thankful for the example Linda has been to me over the years. She is thirty years my senior with much experience. I have willingly welcomed her guidance with great fervor. I hope you have an "Elijah" in your life, too—

someone who is a positive example for you to emulate, someone who is not afraid to correct you by speaking the truth with love. She will also laugh with you until your sides split and cry with you at the drop of a phone call. She will lead you to Jesus and away from herself and always offer a prayer.

For myself, I have tried to embrace the aging process gracefully like my friend Linda because I know everyone isn't privileged to grow older. You see, there was a time I wasn't sure I would have the opportunity to live beyond my thirties. My plea to the Lord was to allow me to live long enough to raise my daughters. Each day that passes has been a gift from God, and now I am enjoying the next generation.

The Lord never designed a generation to operate apart from its parents and grandparents. Nor did He design the parents and grandparents to halt the march of progress they themselves pushed so hard to create. It's not just the younger generation who are "fresh and green," though they have youth on their side, but the older generation, who have decades of experiencing God's faithfulness and goodness.[2]

I want to be like the psalmist's proclamation in Psalm 92:12-15:

> *The righteous man will flourish*
> *like the palm tree,*
> *He will grow like a cedar in Lebanon.*

> *Planted in the house of the Lord,*
> *They will flourish in the courts of our God.*
> *They will still yield fruit in old age;*
> *They shall be full of sap and very green,*
> *To declare that the Lord is upright;*
> He is *my rock, and there is no*
> *unrighteousness in Him.*

Psalm 92:12-15 is a beautiful picture of a person who has willfully and sincerely repented of their sins, accepted the Lord Jesus as their personal Savior, and in turn wears the label of *righteous* and *godly*. This seems like a high and lofty label to wear, but your loving Father pins it on you when you desire to live a life fully devoted to Him.

Thankfully, He restores your soul and guides you in the paths of His righteousness for His name's sake (Psalm 23:3). God promises that a righteous life will flourish and grow: "For the eyes of the Lord move to and fro throughout the earth that He may strongly support those whose heart is completely His" (2 Chronicles 16:9).

God's desire is that you will move into a "wholehearted" lifestyle—one devoted fully to Him, producing much fruit. We can learn volumes from the beautiful illustration of the palm tree and the cedar in Lebanon. As depicted in Psalm 92, they bear much fruit. Specifically, palm trees grow deep roots into the ground until they strike living springs so they can later display a towering beauty. And when strong winds come, the root system of the palm tree is not weakened but actually strengthened by these storms! May you grow deep roots in Christ, drawing nourishment from Him for your daily living and being able to live above your circumstances with a towering beauty for others to see the strength of the Lord. When you have a secure root system in place, it will help you survive the storms.

Along the same lines, cedar trees are strong and mighty. May you bear the unbending strength of a cedar as you call upon the name of the Lord for your power. Your flourishing and growth will continue into old age as you seek God for nourishment and might.

My dear friend Linda battled COVID at the age of eighty-five with great strength and vigor—much like the palm and cedar tree. I have watched her embrace a new normal with very little "woe is me" attitude. Yes, we have all observed her transition and grown from it. Change is never easy, but if we accept a new season of life with gratitude, it helps us move on and look at the future with brighter eyes and a desire for new opportunities.

So, let's embrace the days in front of us with a grateful heart and display a "green olive tree" lifestyle because we are planted in the presence of God. And let us not forget what God treasures: a surpassing devotion to Him, which is represented by a life fully committed to Him. If you and I forget what God treasures, we will lack the in-filling of joy, peace, and love.

Reflection Questions

1. Which of the four steps of living a "green olive tree" lifestyle will you need to embrace in this season of your life: live in the presence of God, trust in the steadfast love of God, express thankfulness, or wait patiently on the Lord?

2. Has your life turned out the way you thought it would? If not, will you embrace the road before you and accept the challenge to embrace what God has planned?

3. Do you have an "Elijah"—a guide and leader in your life? Share what the relationship provides for you.

4. Are you an "Elijah" in the life of another woman? Share what the relationship provides for you.

Eight
The Power of Positive Thinking

This chapter may not be the end-all fix to having a positive attitude, but I do hope that it will be the catalyst to a more positive approach to your everyday living. There is definitely something to be said about the person who looks at a glass as half-full versus the one with a half-empty attitude. Stop for a minute and ask yourself who would you rather be around, a positive or negative person? I think the answer is pretty obvious—a positive person. So, if that's the case, then let's strive to be that positive person in the lives of others.

A positive attitude will be a necessary quality you will need to be intentional about displaying, and there may even be some days you'll feel like you have to fake it until you make it. There's no doubt about it . . . I am always drawn to positive, upbeat Christians. They seem to display the character of God in any situation and help draw me closer to the heart of my Savior—Jesus Christ. They help to make the path ahead more clear and bright.

When writing the book, this is one of the last chapters I tackled. I was coached early on in my writing career to start with the chapters that come the easiest and then work toward the more difficult ones. Most of the chapters in this book were born from my monthly blog written during the pandemic. Unbeknownst to me, a thread of perspective ran through the content of each blog. God was writing this book before I knew I would pen the first word.

But not this chapter. Nope. This one was different and stood alone for me. God knew I would write this chapter from living in the experience of finding positivity. I am actually writing most of this chapter from my bed. Yes, you heard me, from my bed . . . between watching the Hallmark channel and taking naps.

It was the day after Thanksgiving 2021 that I found out I tested positive for COVID. Even though I was fully vaccinated and had taken so many precautionary measures, I couldn't dodge the virus. The hardest reality of the entire experience was that my daughter's family with her two-week-old baby and a two-and-a-half year old were with us for the holiday. There wasn't much of a positive vibe in the air upon the announcement. This was one of those situations where I was going to have to dig deep to find anything positive at all. If I am honest, I was in a bad place emotionally and spiritually. What did this mean for me, and what did it mean for our family?

Thankfully, one of the reads on my bedroom side-table was John Gordon's book, *The Positive Dog*, an inspiring, heartwarming fictional story that not only reveals the strategies and benefits of being positive but also emphasizes an essential truth for humans: Being positive doesn't just make you better. It makes everyone around you better. Gordon tells the story that we all have two dogs inside of us. One dog is positive, happy, optimistic, and hopeful. The other dog is negative, mad, sad, pessimistic, and fearful. These two dogs often fight inside us, but guess who wins the fight? The one you feed the most.[1]

For the weeks leading up to this unfortunate situation, I kept saying to my husband, "Just feed the positive dog." There were small incidents when I needed to practice what I was reading, but this one seemed to be bigger than I could handle—COVID. I was going to have to put into practice not just what I read but also what I teach others.

So I started with what I knew best: Scripture, prayer, song, family, and friends. And I began to look at this "down-time" as a way to finish this manuscript . . . well, at least this chapter. Yes, this was the silver lining in all of this unfortunate situation. When you and I hit a rough patch, and there seems to be only negativity hovering over us like a dismal cloud that won't let the sun beam through, we must replace negative thoughts with positive and inspiring words. John 10:10 says, "The thief comes only to steal and kill and destroy; I [Jesus] came so that they would have life, and have it abundantly." The evil one doesn't want you to live a victorious and fruitful life. He wants you to remain stuck; however, we have a better Advocate on our side that is always fighting and praying for us. You and I must not allow Satan to stunt our growth, but rather allow Jesus to strengthen us through His power, which mightily works within us (Colossians 1:29).

Philippians 4:7-9 (NLT) is where we need to turn our attention:

> *Then you will experience God's peace, which*
> *exceeds anything we can understand. His peace*
> *will guard your hearts and minds as you live*
> *in Christ Jesus. And now, dear brothers and*
> *sisters, one final thing. Fix your thoughts*
> *on what is true, and honorable, and right,*
> *and pure, and lovely, and admirable. Think*
> *about things that are excellent and worthy*
> *of praise. Keep putting into practice all you*
> *learned and received from me—everything*
> *you heard from me and saw me doing.*
> *Then the God of peace will be with you.*

True. Honorable. Right. Pure. Lovely. Admirable. These words are all found under the positivity category and where our thoughts must rest. But how do we stop the downward spiral long enough to look up? Stop. Drop. Breathe. Pray. Let go.

- *Stop* what you're doing. Stop how you're thinking.
- *Drop* to your knees and pray.
- *Breathe* in deeply God's love for you.
- *Let go* of the negative vibes and replace them with God's Word of truth and love.
- *Let go* of all those emotions that absolutely have no positive effects on your life.

And repeat this process as often as needed, which may be every minute at first. But that's okay!

Sometimes, you may need to remove yourself from the situation and step outside. Yes, literally—go for a walk or listen to a song that washes over you and soothes your soul. A daily walk is a non-negotiable in my day. Even if it's a short walk, it's still a time to break away from the minutiae of issues that can bring me down, help me clear my head, and allow me to view the situation from a different angle.

You become what controls your mind. "For as he thinks within himself, so he is" (Proverbs 23:7a). Period. This Scripture from Proverbs speaks truth. Do you tend to believe negative thoughts about yourself or a particular situation? Maybe they are thoughts you have repeatedly played in your mind, such as lies that other people have spoken to you or wrongs that haunt you. Regardless of what these negative thoughts are, you have believed them for too long.

The great news is that when you confess them as sin to God, you're forgiven. You must allow the Word of God to mold you, ignoring the lies that infiltrate your mind. If you want to change your thinking, get into God's Word and renew your mind. Feeding your mind with truth is a continual process that will change you from the inside out.

Choosing not to renew your mind may actually keep you from fulfilling the purposes and callings of God. In the end, your life moves in the direction of your strongest thoughts. When you change your thinking, you change your direction. "But let God transform you into a new person by changing the way you think. Then you will learn to know God's will for you, which is good and pleasing and perfect" (Romans 12:2 NLT).

The word "renew" means to replace something old with something new—a complete change. It's the discarding of old information not by the process of erasure but by the process of replacement. Only as you guard your heart with God's Word can those old thoughts be replaced with new beliefs that will glorify God. Philippians 4:7-9 promises peace to people who practice right thinking.

If you replace negative talk with positive truth, God will guard your heart and mind with what He thinks about you. "Your eyes saw me when I was formless; all my days were written in your book and planned before a single one of them began. God, how precious your thoughts are to me; how vast their sum is! (Psalm 139:16-17 ESV). Right thinking begins with the words you speak to yourself and where your thoughts are fixed—on what is true, honorable, right, pure, lovely, admirable, excellent, and worthy of praise. It's time to stop the cycle of wrong thinking. Instead, start dwelling on the truths of God and allow His promise of peace to wash over your mind.

Another critical key to achieving a positive mindset is to surround yourself with people who will uplift you and not bring you down. There will always be people you thought would be your biggest fans, yet they have become your biggest frustrations. You will want to walk away from those who won't help move you forward. Please don't misunderstand me: I am not saying you can't have others who speak hard truths into your life, but just make sure they are people who want to help you become a better version of yourself. They may speak hard truths, but they do it with a loving and restorative spirit, using words that bring revival and validity.

Without friends, you will not only fall, but you will become extremely lonely. In my book, *Friendship Sisters for a Journey*, I dedicated a whole chapter to a term I call "sistering." Sistering occurs when two women come together to share their hearts and lives. After their time together, each one believes she was the one who got the greatest blessing. Soon after I wrote this chapter and offered a conference on friendship, a woman came up to me and asked, "Did you know 'sistering' is a carpentry term, too?" No, I didn't.

You know it . . . . I went right home to start researching the word and found the parallel—"riveting." When you sister a beam, floor joint, or pillar, you add extra material to strengthen damaged material. You normally can't remove the damaged beam, so you add strength to the existing beam on either side. Just as with a damaged beam, when a hurting friend needs encouragement, you surround her with strong women on either side who will strengthen and support her for what lies ahead.

Two are good because you have a friend who can assist, but three are even better, for a triple-braided cord is not easily broken. Ecclesiastes 4:9-12 (NLT) says,

> *Two people are better off than one, for they*
> *can help each other succeed. If one person*
> *falls, the other can reach out and help. But*
> *someone who falls alone is in real trouble.*
> *Likewise, two people lying close together can*

*keep each other warm. But how can one be
warm alone? A person standing alone can be
attacked and defeated, but two can stand back-
to-back and conquer. Three are even better,
for a triple-braided cord is not easily broken.*

You can have the full body of armor on and stand firm:

- Buckle the belt of truth around your waist.
- Set the breastplate of righteousness in place.
- Fit your feet with the readiness that comes from the gospel of peace.
- Take up the shield of faith, with which you can extinguish all the flaming arrows of the evil one.
- Put on the helmet of salvation.
- Wield the sword of the Spirit, which is the Word of God.

But at the same time, you still have your backside uncovered (Ephesians 6:10-17). As you look at Ecclesiastes 4:9-12, you will see that when two believers come together with the full armor of God on and standing back-to-back, they can conquer whatever is in front of them. They will be completely covered on all sides, even their backs.

Yet the most important piece of the armor is prayer. Ephesians 6:18a says, "With all prayer and supplication pray at all times in the Spirit." If you have a faithful praying sister upholding you, you are a fortunate and blessed girl. Prayer is the catalyst of a strong friendship.

So, you must allow others to join you. Uphold you. Carry you. Encourage you . . . and sometimes drag you. This is *sistering* at its best.

Although we are hit with negative thoughts and situations at times, we can't allow them to consume us. Thinking positively is good for your soul, both physically and spiritually.

I love reading Winnie the Pooh books to my grandsons. There are so many great life lessons we can learn from that little yellow fictional teddy bear. Pooh gave Christopher Robin the mantra: "You're braver than you believe, and stronger than you seem, and smarter than you think." This is a great phrase to repeat to yourself and others who need a word of encouragement in any new or uncomfortable situation that arises.

Having someone who believes in you or sees something in you that you struggle to see in yourself will be key to moving you forward. Positivity changes your demeanor. It turns a frown upside down. It puts a sparkle back in your eye and a skip in your walk. No matter what you have experienced, you can move forward when you have the support of others.

Let me share a personal story with you that changed the trajectory of my life and ministry. I recall a time when God opened a door of opportunity to something that I thought would be the most amazing experience. And yes, it started out that way. But soon after that, it slowly started to spiral out of control, to the point that I stepped away one week out from the event, along with a few others.

Leadership styles looked very different from the time I began the quest. It was an eighteen-month commitment that didn't end the way I expected. Or, was it exactly what God ordered?

I vividly remember coming home from the meeting after I resigned and walking into a dark house. My husband had already been tucked into bed for many hours. Honestly, I didn't have the heart to wake him, especially since he had pleaded with me six months earlier to step away. These were his exact words: "You will pull out one week before the event." I thought to myself, *Whaaat? No way. I am doing this for God and not for man. I can do this for the betterment of our community and local women.* So, I marched on . . . .

That heartbreaking night when I resigned, I took my spot on the family room couch and vowed to never do ministry again. Never, I said to myself. The long night soon came to an end with the breaking of dawn. The following days were difficult, but the presence of God and a few friends helped me to continue ahead and hold my head above water.

The event came and went, and if you are wondering, I did attend the event along with forty-eight hundred other women. It was a success, and our community was forever changed by His spoken word. So, what man meant for harm, God meant for good.

This experience drove me to wholeheartedly seek my biggest influencer, Jesus Christ.

It changed the trajectory of whom and how closely I followed. It became more about pleasing God rather than pleasing man. Once I refocused my sight and fixed my eyes back on Him, the author and perfecter of my faith, there was clarity. Yes, Jesus is the example, but He will also surround you with others to encourage you, teach you, and keep pointing you to Him.

The silver lining of this experience was having a dear acquaintance-turned-mentor rise up to come alongside me and spur me on. She was a true portrait of what servant leadership looked like in the midst of chaos. On the day of that challenging event I just shared with you, she was the one who viewed me across the field on my morning walk. After pulling over and parking her PT Cruiser, she walked over to me and cupped my face in her hands to speak truth into my aching heart. She was the one who could see potential in this young woman when I could barely see two feet in front of me. I learned the heart of Jesus and the power of sistering. The more time I spent with her, the more I fell in love with Jesus.

Not only was my relationship with Christ transformed, but I learned that whom you follow matters. Do they direct you to Jesus or themselves? Are they "I am here," or "There you are" kind of people? In other words, do they lead their followers selfishly, or selflessly?

From that life-changing morning walk, I have set out to be that person who seeks out others and positively encourages them in their calling, walk, and life. I want to emulate the actions of my dear friend and be that positive bright hope in another's life. I don't always get it right, but I keep working on it and so can you! Choosing to be positive will not only change your life, but the lives of others.

And I just want to close this chapter with an update on our COVID dilemma . . . . Yes, we all had it—me, my husband, my daughter's family, and many of our extended family, but thankfully we came through it counting our blessings and holding each other a little closer.

Reflection Questions

1. Share how this book has helped you to gain a more positive outlook.

2. Do you have friends who are able to help sustain you, encourage you, and come alongside you in a sistering manner?

3. What qualities of your friends do you want to emulate?

4. How are you trying to remove the negative talk that may be taking up too much space in your life?

Nine
Walking After Emptiness

Have you ever heard of the phrase, "walking after emptiness"? Well, it was new for me too. While I was reading the Book of Jeremiah, this phrase jumped out at me. In Jeremiah 2:5 the Lord asks, "What injustice did your fathers find in Me, that they went far from Me, and walked after emptiness and became empty?"

What does "walking after emptiness" actually mean? We are either walking after emptiness or fullness. "Walk" is the biblical expression for fellowship and obedience that is lived out through our actions. "To walk" can be translated "to live." Just as the Israelites sought after empty idols as their guide, you and I can do the same in our daily lives as we walk after things that don't fulfill us. If you and I walk after emptiness, we will become empty. Whatever we walk after, we become.

What does walking after emptiness look like in today's culture, and are these some areas of worldly pursuit?

- Embracing a world view
- Seeking vanity that won't last
- Striving for power
- Desiring fame
- Social media status
- The love of money
- And more . . .

Jeremiah 7:23-24 continues to say, "But this is what I command them, saying, 'Obey My voice, and I will be your God, and you will be My people; and you will walk in all the way which I command you, that it may be well with you.' Yet they did not obey or incline their ear, but walked in their own counsels, and in the stubbornness of their evil heart, and went backward and not forward." Similarly, Asaph, in Psalm 81:11-12, shares what will happen to the Israelites if they do not listen to God: "But My people did not listen to My voice, and Israel did not obey Me. So I gave them over to the stubbornness of their heart, to walk in their own devices."

If you and I want to move forward and not backward, we should live in a way that honors and pleases God— with a willing ear to listen to His precepts. Proverbs 2 is a guide to walking upright. Verse 7b says that if we heed God's instruction, "He will be a shield to those who walk in integrity." Verse 1 tells us to treasure His commandments. Verse 2 exhorts us to incline our hearts to understanding. Verse 4 urges us to seek and search for wisdom. Yes, this will take a concentrated effort on our part to pursue and acquire wisdom from God, but it will guard and watch over us (v. 11) and help keep us on the right path (v. 20).

These three words—*if, then,* and *but*—make a transformational difference in our lives and can sway our direction. They are a part of conditional statements: "If you do this . . . then this will happen. But, if you continue this way . . . then this will happen." The way we respond to conditional statements will be a part of our journey toward God or away from Him—walking after emptiness or fullness. It is our individual choice. In the words of Joshua, "Choose for yourselves today whom you will serve" (Joshua 24:15).

Specifically, the little word "if" has a big impact throughout the Word of God. We see it appear in Scripture almost sixteen hundred times between the opening of the Old Testament book of Genesis to the last New Testament book of Revelation.[1] Repeatedly in Scripture, we find God's conditional "if and then" scenarios that lead to optional outcomes. I find encouragement to follow God's ways in the Book of Deuteronomy, and I make sure to read it at the beginning of every year. Moses is a straight shooter with the blessings and curses of God. However, I must preface this by saying that we serve a grace-filled God whose offer of salvation is free and unconditional: "For this is how God loved the world: He gave His one and only Son, so that everyone who believes in Him will not perish but have eternal life" (John 3:16 NLT).

Throughout Deuteronomy Moses, while giving the Israelites their final instruction in his last days on earth, shares the blessings and curses that come from their obedience or lack of it. Deuteronomy 28 gives a perfect example of God's conditional blessings and curses. The first fourteen verses outline His blessings for those who hear, obey, and follow Him. Moses says, "Now it shall be, *if* you diligently obey the Lord your God, being careful to do all His commandments which I am commanding you today, that the Lord your God will put you high above all the nations of the earth. And all these blessings will come to you and reach you *if* you obey the Lord your God" (vv. 1-2, emphasis author). Blessings will come to them in their land, work, home, and offspring if they obey God's ways, statutes, and commandments (vv. 3-14).

So are these conditional statements just for those in the Old Testament? No! They are just as meaningful for us today as they were back then. We would be wise to heed the instruction from the early men and women of faith. Although some blessings are specifically meant for the Israelites, God also bestows blessings upon all of us. Nevertheless, there are still conditions tied to the blessings.

These are some "if" blessings from the New Testament:

*"Then Jesus said to His disciples, 'If anyone
wants to become My follower, he must deny
himself, take up his cross, and follow Me.
For whoever wants to save his life will
lose it, but whoever loses his life because
of Me will find it. For what does it benefit
a person if he gains the whole world but
forfeits his life? Or what can a person
give in exchange for his life?'"*
(Matthew 16:24-26 NET)

*"'If you remain in Me, and My words
remain in you, ask whatever you wish,
and it will be done for you.'"*
(John 15:7 NIV)

*"'You are My friends if you do
what I command you.'"*
(John 15:14 ESV)

*Now by this we know that we know Him, if we
keep His commandments. He who says, 'I know
Him,' and does not keep His commandments,
is a liar, and the truth is not in him. But
whoever keeps His word, truly the love of God
is perfected in him. By this we know that we*

> *are in Him. He who says he abides in Him*
> *ought himself also to walk just as He walked.*
> (1 John 2:3-6 NKJV)

> *"And a third angel followed them and spoke*
> *with a loud voice: 'If anyone worships the*
> *beast and his image and receives a mark on*
> *his forehead or on his hand, he will also drink*
> *the wine of God's wrath, which is mixed full*
> *strength in the cup of His anger. He will be*
> *tormented with fire and sulfur in the sight of*
> *the holy angels and in the sight of the Lamb.'"*
> (Revelation 14:9-10 HCSB)

There are times you and I have fallen short of the glory of God and have walked our own way. But thankfully we have a God who unconditionally loves us (Romans 8:37-39) and provides second chances for us. God is for you (Psalm 56:9b). Yes, how great it is to serve a God who gives salvation with no ifs, thens, or buts—thankfully, eternal love is unconditional! However, the blessings He gives us throughout our time on Earth directly correlate to the choices we make.

Whether experiencing God's love through reward or discipline, you can know that He wants the best for you and that, "[He] has come that you may have life, and that you may have it more abundantly" (John 10:10 NKJV).

But ultimately it is your choice how you will live your day—walking in His ways or not. In some moments, you might take one step forward and two steps back. Or, maybe what others meant for harm really will benefit you for good. Keep moving. Keep seeking Him. Keep looking up. Allow Him to fill your thoughts and illuminate your path. He will make the way clearer. Psalm 16:11 says, "In His presence is fullness of joy."

Yes, it's your choice—will you choose life and obedience, or walk after emptiness?

> *"But the message is very near you, in your*
> *mouth and in your heart, so that you may*
> *follow it. See, today I have set before you life*
> *and prosperity, death and adversity. For I*
> *am commanding you today to love the Lord*
> *your God, to walk in His ways, and to keep*
> *His commands, statutes, and ordinances, so*
> *that you may live and multiply, and the Lord*
> *your God may bless you in the land you are*
> *entering to possess. But if your heart turns*
> *away and you do not listen and you are led*
> *astray to bow down to other gods and worship*
> *them, I tell you today that you will certainly*
> *perish and will not live long in the land you*
> *are entering to possess across the Jordan. I*
> *call heaven and earth as witnesses against you*

> *today that I have set before you life and death,*
> *blessing and curse. Choose life so that you*
> *and your descendants may live, love the Lord*
> *your God, obey Him, and remain faithful to*
> *Him. For He is your life, and He will prolong*
> *your life in the land the Lord swore to give to*
> *your fathers Abraham, Isaac, and Jacob."*

(Deuteronomy 30:14-20 HCSB, emphasis author)

Some years back, I found myself doubting my commitment to God. It wasn't that I walked away or was intentionally walking after emptiness. Instead, it was a time when doubt reared its ugly head and wreaked havoc on my thoughts . . . . *Was I truly a follower of Christ? Did I believe all of Scripture?* But then while reading First John 2, I found reassurance that what my heart desired was to know Him better, walk in obedience to His ways, and abide in Him (1 John 2:3-6). After reading these verses, instantly I knew I was His and was able to stop doubting my allegiance. I might not always do it or get it right, but I keep striving to please Him and choose daily to live for Him. And so can you—one day at a time! So what will your choice be for today? *If* you do _____, *then* what _____?

Ephesians 4:1 challenges us to walk after fullness: "Therefore I, the prisoner of the Lord, implore you to walk in a manner worthy of the calling with which you have been called."

Walking worthy of the Lord is a step-by-step process, one that begins by just focusing on the next step. Sometimes we become discouraged in the process because seeking victory seems overwhelming. Yet, if we desire to be the people God wants us to be, our focus only needs to be on the next step—and nothing else. We must walk moment by moment, hour by hour, and then day by day. Yes, we should have the end goal in view, but all He asks of us is to take the next step. We must be obedient to what He is asking for the day before us, and He promises to care for what lies ahead.

You remember my friend, Linda, whom I shared about with you in Chapter Seven, 'Living a 'Green Olive Tree' Life"? Well, I have had a front-row seat to her life for many years and have watched her live life to the fullest with her days. She seems to be right where her feet are, from being intentional with her family to the needs of her church family and ministry partners. However, viewing her life while battling COVID at the ripe age of eighty-five has taught all of us another life lesson. Thankfully she came through the virus, but life looked different for her post-hospital stay. She found herself moving out of her very independent life and apartment into her daughter's home for many months until she was able to get back on her recovered, stable feet. Once she was able to return to a more autonomous lifestyle and settled into her independent living community, she was discovered.

Because she received this new way of life with an open mind and eyes to see what God was doing right where she was, she excelled—people were drawn to the Jesus in her. She started a Bible study, joined the shuffleboard competition, and brought vitality to the others around her. She would say to me, "I never thought this is where I would be, but since I am, I need to make the best of it and live for God right where I am—it's the biggest mission field I have ever seen and the nicest people I have ever known." Linda became an example to all of us to just take the next step, and then God will take care of the steps that follow.

Be watchful and obedient right where you are placed and have a Christ-like attitude while living life, even if it's not what you expected. Allow God to write your story and watch Him show off. Oh, by the way, that's not all of Linda's story. As I write this chapter, the leaders of the independent living facility where Linda lives have appointed her to be the resident association president of the community.

Although Linda was trying to walk worthy of the Lord, she felt at times that success was elusive. Just like Linda, you probably find yourself good for a few days but then get tripped up. Remember though, you are in the process of perfecting your walk. You are no different from anyone else. In fact, we all need the same power that comes from Christ to walk worthy of the Lord. It is His divine power that enables us!

Herein lies our *walk*—emulating Christ's character in how we live. It is what drives our purpose. It is our true north. What we believe deep in our core will dictate how we walk, affect our responses, and determine our motives. You and I become whatever and whoever we hold in high esteem.

Second Corinthians 3:18 states, "But we all, with unveiled face, beholding as in a mirror the glory of the Lord, are being transformed into the same image from glory to glory, just as from the Lord, the Spirit." One of the greatest characteristics we can exhibit is a completely exposed openness before God, which will allow our lives to become a mirror for others. Removal of the veil gives us access to God, and then we can constantly reflect Christ's divine glory, which transforms us from glory to glory, making us more and more like Him as we are changed into His glorious image.

There is nothing between us and God. Psalm 34:5 (NLT) says, "[When you] look to Him for help [you] will be radiant with joy; no shadow of shame will darken [your] faces." Yes, it takes a deliberate act of exposure to the Father. You and I need to continually make it a priority to enter the secret place and walk it out with God. And when we do, He is able to change our approach, attitude, demeanor, and desire.

After reading this chapter, how would you describe your walk? Is it one in pursuit of emptiness—or fullness? You and I can't change our past, but we can choose our future. You can choose from this day forward to strive for excellence and commit your days to the One who holds your future.

> *Not that I have already obtained it or have*
> *already become perfect, but I press on so that*
> *I may lay hold of that for which also I was*
> *laid hold of by Christ Jesus. Brethren, I do*
> *not regard myself as having laid hold of it*
> *yet; but one thing I do: forgetting what lies*
> *behind and reaching forward to what lies*
> *ahead, I press on toward the goal for the prize*
> *of the upward call of God in Christ Jesus.*
> (Philippians 3:12-14)

Press on. Reach forward toward the goal, your upward call. These words are encouragement for your movement to be forward, not backward. Continue to walk in fullness and leave emptiness at the back door, not seeking fulfillment from the world but rather from God.

Reflection
Questions

1. After reading this chapter, how would you describe your walk? Is it one in pursuit of emptiness, or fullness?

2. Do you find yourself walking after emptiness? What will it take for you to walk in the fullness of God?

3. Which of the if blessings encouraged you, from pages 119-120? So what will your choice be for today? If you do _____, then what _____?

Ten
Stop and Pick the Raspberries

L et me preface this chapter by saying that no one needs this challenge more than I do. The title of this chapter came during my daily walk, which I've always considered my respite time of day.

There aren't many days I miss a walk. We even bundle up and hit the snowy streets when necessary. It's my main form of exercise since the age of thirty-nine after having my left lung removed due to Cushing's syndrome.

Some walks are by myself. Some days they're with my husband or friends, but mostly with my furry friends—Baxter and Murphy. There are days it's purely a prayer walk; other walks involve listening to a podcast or calling my mentor, mom, or friend.

However, on this particular summer day while I was walking by myself, the wild raspberries were ready for picking along the path, and I am a sap for not passing them up. But while picking them, I kept saying to myself, *I don't have time to pick these today.* Right before I stopped to pick, I was listening to a book on Audible. The author shared about rest, and I realized some of my walks weren't really relaxing at all. Let me just stop right now and say that this caught me totally off guard. What I thought was a breather in my day a lot of times was just a continuation of my work. Now, don't get me wrong. I continue to listen to podcasts and walk with friends. However, it was more of a mindset shift to enjoy the walk, and some days to just walk in silence—stopping and picking the raspberries without feeling guilty for being still.

I was reminded again while reading the second chapter of Genesis that God is the creator of rest, "By the seventh day God completed His work which He had done, and He rested on the seventh day from all His work which He had done. Then God blessed the seventh day and sanctified it, because in it He rested from all His work which God had created and made" (Genesis 2:2-3). Even God rested. How much more should we make sure to leave margin to rest?

Being still is hard for most of us in the twenty-first century, but discovering rest will energize us and fuel our tired souls for what lies ahead. Finding rest can vary from taking an afternoon siesta to sitting in a rocking chair on the porch with a glass of sweet tea in hand, or whatever stops your motion for a period of time. The hard part to exercising rest is implementing stillness and remaining consistent. Is exercising rest an oxymoron? When I wrote the phrase, "exercising rest," I thought I may need to edit it, but no. Because we definitely need to practice the art of resting.

Hebrews 4:11 confirms this: "Therefore let us be diligent to enter that rest, so that no one will fall, through *following* the same example of disobedience." Yes, it will take a concentrated effort on your part and willingness to stop and pick the raspberries, and smell the roses. In other words, seize the day. Life is short. Don't miss the opportunity to enjoy the fruit of your labor and daily rest in the arms of Jesus.

St. Augustine wrote in his book *Confessions*, "You have made us for Yourself, oh God; and our hearts are restless until they rest in You." Aren't there days when you seem to wrestle with the idea of stopping, and you never quite achieve what you have set out to do . . . like rest? Yup, me too.

Many of us can quote Psalm 46:10 (NIV): "Be still, and know I am God." However, I like the NASB version, "Cease striving and know that I am God.""Cease" means to sink, relax, or withdraw.[1] It suggests the image of a person sinking down into a chair in order to relax. You can picture it, right? That comfy-cozy chair you love to recline in while wrapped in your favorite blanket—you settle down to rest, read, or binge-watch Hallmark movies. It's where you find relaxation and enjoy peace and calmness. In other words, it's a time to stop and ponder what God has done for you by lowering the noise of the world.

You and I must be intentional in turning down the volume of the world if we want to be able to discern the voice of God more clearly. There are too many distractions that try to hijack our time in His presence if we are not adamant to guard and protect this sacred space. Yes, there are days we grapple with time and ourselves to carve out this ceasing.

I believe this quote from St. Augustine is worth repeating, "Our hearts are restless until they rest in Jesus." My heart also will long for this ceasing all day long if I don't start the day with stillness. Yes, and amen!

Ceasing first thing in the morning will set the stage for the rest of your day and launch you off on the right path. Even if it's for ten minutes, it will be a high in your day. On other days you may linger for longer periods of time. You know what you need. It's just a matter of carving out the time to be still in His presence. Psalm 5:3 says, "In the morning, O Lord, You will hear my voice; in the morning I will order my prayer to You and eagerly watch." Is your voice the first sound the Lord hears? Or is it Google, Facebook, Instagram, or some other form of social media? It's easy to be drawn into the virtual world or a quick read of the book-of-the-month on your table. Distraction can be very subtle and not a bad thing, but the next thing you know, you are fully engulfed in the things of the world rather than seeking Him.

Our priority should be to seek first His kingdom, and His righteousness (Matthew 6:33). Yes, the Lord wants to have fellowship with us, but He will not force a relationship upon us. The choice is ours for the taking. It must be our daily choice to seek Him and allow His guidance in the quietness of our moments with Him.

If you have allowed the busyness of the day and daily demands of life to invade your space that once was reserved for the Lord, what next? Take a deep breath and start over. It's okay, God has not moved. No, He has not moved, but you can fall away from a closeness you once enjoyed.

I love the description of God revealing Himself to you in *Tony Evans' Study Bible* from John 14:21: "The one who has My commandments and keeps them is the one who loves Me; and the one who loves Me will be loved by My Father, and I will love him and will reveal Myself to him." Tony explains this verse,

> When you are connected to the love of the Father and Son in obedience, Jesus promises to reveal more of Himself to you. If you listen to a radio station in your car, you know the further you get from the broadcast station, the worse your reception of the signal gets. Many people have difficulty connecting with God because

> they've wandered too far away to pick up His
> signal. But if you come back home in obedience,
> relating to God through Christ in love, He will
> disclose more of Himself to you.[2]

The more you reveal yourself to Jesus, the more He will reveal Himself to you.

In Matthew 11:28-29, Jesus tells us, "Come to Me, all who are weary and heavy-laden, and I will give you rest. Take My yoke upon you and learn from Me, for I am gentle and humble in heart, and you will find rest for your souls." In other words, He's saying, "Come to me and find rest." I know this can be a difficult concept to grasp and perform. God promises rest to those who will come, seek, and find it. Cease striving so hard and catch your breath from the daily grind while you refresh your soul in His presence. Breathe in God's presence as you sit quietly before Him and receive His gentle, loving care to help you regain needed strength and rest for your soul.

He wants to meet you in your restlessness that, at times, can overpower you into a frantic frenzy of weariness. He longs to be the stillness deep within your spirit—the hushed strength that overrides the world's expectations. God wants to be the true rest that undergirds your stability in a chaotic world and gives you the ever-present awareness that He is with you, beside you, and all around you, holding you and loving you with His outstretched arms.

The nearness of God will bring satisfaction and stillness to your weary bones. Be still and know He is God. Longing for this rest is a beautiful display of His significance in your life. And as you discover the depths of God through scheduled stillness and focused meditation in His Word, you will become whole. The secret place with God is where you develop an intimate relationship with Him.

Picture an iceberg. The secret place is what happens below the waterline. Under the waterline of an iceberg is a large rock formation, which represents our time with Him. Most of us live our lives without giving much intentional thought to carving out the space necessary to shape lives of love, purpose, meaning, wisdom, and virtue. If you daily meet with God, that undergirding strength will increase, and He will guide you in your everyday choices. It's what happens under the waterline that matters.

The strength you develop as you meet with Jesus will give you the power to walk through your day with confidence. It's just like the Sadducees in the New Testament who witnessed Peter and John teaching in the temple after healing the lame man. Acts 4:13 says, "Now as they observed the confidence of Peter and John and understood that they were uneducated and untrained men, they were amazed, and began to recognize them as having been with Jesus." Yes, it's in the being with Jesus that changes everything, not in the doing. Being with Jesus in the solitude of your day can change your outlook from a low to a high and maybe even a surprising buffalo.

Part of establishing rest will help you realize a vivid appreciation of God's favor and blessing on your life. Are you looking for God's favor in your life? I know there have been times I wished for God to wave a wand over me so His favor would fall on me like rain on parched ground. Oh, wouldn't that be nice? But, that's just wishful thinking. The promise of favor comes when we focus on the three steps written in Proverbs 8:34-35: "Blessed is the man who listens to Me, watching daily at My gates, waiting at My doorposts. For he who finds Me finds life and obtains favor from the Lord."

Yes, to attain everyday favor, the Scripture before us states three prerequisites: listen, watch daily, and wait. Jesus is the gateway to the favor of God. Without God's grace there would be no favor—no blessing from God. Ephesians 2:8 (NIV) says, "For by grace you are saved through faith—and this is not from yourselves, it is the gift of God." Once you have received the gift of life through Jesus' saving blood, His favor doesn't stop. God delights in blessing those who seek Him. He wants to bestow His favor on you daily—*everyday favor.*

Everyday favor is found in your one-on-one time with Him—focusing on Him. The sweetness of His presence will be enough, and the blessings that flow out of your time with Him will be icing on the cake.

There's a desperation in the writer of Proverbs 8:34-35 for more of God, a desire to attain wisdom from above. Do you have this same desperation—that "He must become greater and greater, and I must become less and less" (John 3:30 NLT)? May you and I have this same desperation as we focus our eyes on Him through these three steps to *everyday favor* from Proverbs 8:34-35.

1. Listen.

Listening is a learned art you and I will need to be deliberate about practicing. The way we listen to God is by daily reading His Word and applying its truths, commandments, and wisdom to our lives. We ought to be like Samuel, one of the greatest prophets of Israel, who said, "Speak, for Your servant is listening" (1 Samuel 3:10b). May this be the cry of your heart as well. Don't just merely *hear* Him as noise, but attentively *listen*.

> *"My people, hear my instruction;*
> *listen to the words from my mouth.*
> *I will declare wise sayings;*
> *I will speak mysteries from the past—"*
> (Psalm 78:1-2 CSB)

2. Watch daily.

Are you earnestly knocking on the door of Jesus' heart?
Proverbs 8:17 says, "[God] loves those who love [Him];
and those who diligently seek [Him] will find [Him]."
Don't allow God's Word to become commonplace
whenever you go through your morning devotions in
rote fashion without really listening to what God wants
you to hear from Him and watching for Him throughout
your day. Rather, come to Him each day with a desire
to have your heart stand in awe of His words (Psalm
119:161). Never stop becoming awestruck by God.
Watch for Him daily!

> *"Ask, and it will be given to you; seek,*
> *and you will find; knock, and it will be*
> *opened to you. For everyone who asks*
> *receives, and he who seeks finds, and to*
> *him who knocks it will be opened."*
> (Matthew 7:7-8)

3. Wait.

As you stop and listen to His still small voice, watch
daily and wait expectantly. May you humble yourself
before Him, giving your heart the right posture to listen:
'For God does not delight in the strength of the horse;
He does not take pleasure in the legs of a man. The
Lord favors those who fear Him, those who wait for His

lovingkindness" (Psalm 147:10-11). Be steadfast in your commitment to know Him better, and then watch and wait for our awe-inspiring God to bring favor on your life. During the waiting period, God molds you into the fullness of your destiny and will take you to depths of trust beyond your own understanding. Finding Jesus in the wait is like discovering a treasure brighter than the sparkling of diamonds. He will bring forth a refining that will happen nowhere else but in the waiting. So, embrace the season of waiting and meet Jesus in the middle of it. He is good to those who wait.

> *"The Lord is my portion,' says my soul,*
> *"Therefore I have hope in Him."*
> *The Lord is good to those who wait for*
> *Him, to the person who seeks Him.*
> (Lamentations 3:24-25)

So, press on to know the Lord better and better each day (Hosea 6:3). Rest in His presence. Stop long enough to pick the raspberries and watch for His favor with expectancy. He will be the God who girds you with strength (Psalm 18:32) when you feel weak. He is the God who provides rest to your weary soul. He is your keeper, shade, protector, and guard (Psalm 121:5-8). Rest in these truths, my friend.

Reflection Questions

1. Are there times you struggle with practicing rest?

2. Share how you have embraced rest into your life. What do you do that helps bring revitalization into your days?

3. Which of the three steps do you find the hardest to implement into your day—listen, watch daily, or wait?

4. If needed, what practical step will you take to incorporate rest into your schedule?

Eleven
Control the Controllable

We are living in an unprecedented time when we find ourselves holding our future ministry, events, and life loosely in our hands. The quote from Corrie ten Boom has never rung so clearly then in the present days we are walking through: "Hold loosely to the things of this life so that if God requires them of you, it will be easy to let them go."

I have been asking myself the question, *Is there anything we can control in a time when so many things seem uncontrollable?* You may be asking yourself the same question. Is God asking you to release the control freak that lives in you? I always say, "I am a recovering control freak—I am not yet where I want to be, but I keep striving to let go of trying to control everything." My family nailed it when they bought me a wooden plaque that rests on our fireplace mantel that says, *As long as everything is exactly the way I want it, I am totally flexible.* All joking aside, organizing and planning are not bad characteristics to establish. However, if they block you from seeing beyond your own ideas and not

God's plan for your life, you may want to reconsider the path in front of you.

It seems with the flip of the calendar, another event is being postponed or canceled. An important occasion gets rescheduled or a planned trip is delayed, and with the shifting culture we find ourselves in, there are few things we are able to control. Oh, and how we love to control and plan. As I mentioned, planning is not a bad thing, but what we have come to realize through the pandemic and post-pandemic lifestyle is that with life and leadership comes flexibility! I believe, in theory, we know flexibility is a strong characteristic of a good leader, a committed mom, a faithful friend, and caring co-worker. But oh, how the pandemic we've walked through has caused us to experience flexibility firsthand and take the concept to a new level.

We find ourselves in a very different and new season, a season of loosely planning. And yes, there will be things we are unable to control. But the one thing we always have control over is our attitude. I want to have a Promised-Land attitude like the two spies, Joshua and Caleb, in Numbers 13, which I mentioned in a previous chapter, but want to elaborate on a little more. Moses sent them into Canaan along with the other ten spies to survey the land for forty days. The ten spies had a wilderness attitude of always complaining and seeing only the negative. But Joshua and Caleb were the only two men who had a positive attitude and observed the "no-complaining" rule. They had a yes attitude, along with the faith to see the bigger picture and trust that God had all things under control.

So, like me, you may find yourself needing to believe the truths of Romans 8:28 (NIV) like never before: "And we know that in all things God works for the good of those who love Him, who have been called according to His purpose." God does the work for those who love Him. So what can we control? We can control our love and pursuit for Him! I want to have a whole-hearted lifestyle, one devoted fully to God—don't you?

First Timothy 6:11 gives us a prescription for what we can control: "But flee from these things, you man of God, and pursue righteousness, godliness, faith, love, perseverance and gentleness." Jesus wants to be your priority and focus. Matthew 6:33 tells us to, "seek first His kingdom and His righteousness, and everything else of value will find you." What happens when we control the controllable of righteousness, faith, love, and endurance?

1. First, it's a pursuit! A quest of following Jesus. A journey that needs to be sought daily through a devoted time in God's Word. He becomes your focus.

2. We seek His plans and not our own agenda. In addition, we realize the truths of Psalm 31:14-15, which says, "But as for me, I trust in You, O Lord. I say, 'You are my God.' My times are in Your hand."

3. It unleashes us to become part of the process. We become moldable in His hands and move forward in the calling He sets before us.

4. We keep our eyes focused on Him and not our selfish desires.

5. Our perseverance and endurance comes from a strength beyond ourselves—the working of the Holy Spirit's power.

Controlling the controllable will take incredible commitment on your part. It's not for the faint of heart. So, don't become weary in doing good. Control your pursuit of righteousness by staying committed to God's kingdom, and with intentionality seeking to do His will. Strive to continue on in the strength of the Lord through the Holy Spirit's leading, and persevere! Psalm 37:5 (NLT) tells us, "Commit everything you do to the Lord. Trust Him, and He will help you."

I know, it's easier said than done at times. But again, it comes down to controlling your attitude, mindset, and actions. You cannot allow the attitudes of others to control you. You want to be the difference in the lives of others. You want to be the person that helps others see the light at the end of the tunnel and the rainbow through the storm.

By controlling the controllable, you will actually show the watching world your commitment to Christ. A person can choose to be positive or negative, to be a creator or a complainer, to take responsibility or avoid responsibility. Build on what you do have—strengths and assets—and stop complaining about what you don't have. By seeking Christ, you can display His character of love, joy, peace, patience, kindness, goodness, gentleness, faithfulness, and self-control (Galatians 5:22).

- When everything within you wants to seek revenge, you can show love.

- When you want to crawl up in a ball and not face the day ahead, you can display the joy that comes from your relationship with Christ.

- When the world is crumbling around you with discontent, you can be at peace because you know the God who holds the future.

- When that family member gets under your skin, you can demonstrate patience and show kindness even when it's not deserved.

- When that co-worker speaks a harsh word, you can respond with a gentle answer. Proverbs 15:1 (CSB) says, "A gentle answer turns away anger, but a harsh word stirs up wrath."

- When others around you walk away from their convictions, you can stay faithful with yours and commit your ways to the Lord.

- When your flesh wants to do something not according to God's Word, self-control kicks in because it's the Holy Spirit's control that overrides your fleshly desires.

Oh, wouldn't this be a perfect world if everyone would be controlled by the Spirit? Yes, it's our ambition to be controlled by the Spirit, but there are times we fall short. So, what do we do when we don't live up to the expectations of others, or for that matter, our own convictions? We start over!

God is patient about giving us second chances—and not just one, but continual second chances. Micah 7:18 (NIV) says, "Who is a God like you, who pardons sin and forgives the transgression of the remnant of his inheritance? You do not stay angry forever but delight to show mercy." God savors opportunities to offer second chances and is eager not to punish us when we truly seek forgiveness for our sin (Joel 2:13).

I love the biblical story of Jonah, a man who is running away from the presence and direction of God and gets swallowed up by a whale. God first approached him in Jonah 1:1-2: "The word of the Lord came to Jonah the son of Amattai saying, 'Arise, go to Nineveh, the great city, and cry against it, for their wickedness has come up before me.'" God wanted Jonah to go to the wicked city of Ninevah, but Jonah didn't want the people of that city to be spared because of their evilness. So, he tried to run away from God. (But you can't run away from God. He will find you. Psalm 139:7-8 asks, "Where can I go from Your Spirit? Or where can I flee from Your presence?")

While Jonah was at sea, the ship he was aboard experienced a storm, and Jonah realized their great demise was because of him. So he suggested that the crew throw him into the raging ocean. Once the sailors did as Jonah asked, they experienced calm waters. Then, a great fish swallowed Jonah, where he remained for three days. While fainting in the belly of the fish, Jonah remembered the Lord and prayed to God (Jonah 2:7). "Then the Lord commanded the fish, and it vomited Jonah up onto dry land" (v. 10 NIV). And here's the beautiful redemption of God in Jonah 3:1-3, "Now the word of the Lord came to Jonah the second time, saying, 'Arise, go to Nineveh, the great city, and proclaim to it the proclamation which I am going to tell you.' So Jonah arose and went." Jonah got a second chance to redeem himself and be obedient to God. And so can you!

My question is, what are you doing with the second chance you have been given? Are you living your life to the fullest? Are you glorifying God with your days on Earth? He wants to use you. He wants your days to count. You and I want our lives to matter, leaving our mark on this generation and the next.

We want to live abundant lives empowered by the Holy Spirit. However, before we can produce anything, we must first be connected to the main source who does the increasing. In the Gospel of John, Jesus speaks of Himself as the vine, which is actually His last "I am" statement of the seven recorded in Scripture (John 15:1). The *true* vine in the vineyard is the essential trunk of the vine, and on the vine are many branches. Some branches are plentiful, while others produce little to no fruit. This imagery portrays Jesus as the main trunk and you and I as the branches. Separate from Him we are unable to produce lasting fruit. He is the source of all our lives and every good thing we do. Without this connection, we are incapable of living an empowered life. Apart from Him, we can do nothing. Power comes from the Vine, not the branches. To live a purposeful, fruitful, and empowered life, we must be rooted in the depths of God.

As we have already established, we will want to spend concentrated time with the Lord in the stillness of our day. For when we make Him our main delight, He will multiply our efforts. He made each one of us full of great potential and purpose. He made us to be fruitful, producing only what brings Him glory. Too many times, we rush through the abiding process and charge ahead to the end product, all the while wondering why things aren't working for our good.

Because you have been made alive with Jesus (Colossians 2:13), together with Him you can accomplish great things. Yes, you and I want our lives to matter and tell the next generation the praises of the Lord, His strength, and the wondrous works He has done (Psalm 78:4)! God has kept you alive and given you opportunity for fruitful living. Yes, fruitful living! Although there may be days when you feel slightly sluggish, God is in the business of breathing breath into your lungs, so that you may come *alive* and know that He is the Lord (Ezekiel 37:6).

In John 14:12, Jesus' words should encourage us to continue the works of God when He tells us, "'Truly, truly, I say to you, he who believes in Me, the works that I do, he will do also; and greater works than these he will do; because I go to the Father.'" When Jesus went to be with His Father, He left the Holy Spirit to dwell both in the disciples and us, which would enable our works to have the ability to reach farther, with greater quality and impact. The reality is that we need to do the work available to us. Others can see the gospel advance in and through us in greater ways than ever before. Through faith in Him and the indwelling Spirit of God, we have the power and the provision to be effective in a supernatural way.

Psalm 1:2-3 (NLT) gives you three purposeful components to abundant living: "But they delight in the law of the Lord, meditating on it day and night. They are like trees planted along the riverbank, bearing fruit each season. Their leaves never wither, and they prosper in all they do." So, you must actively carry out these principles: 1) delight in the Lord; 2) meditate on His Word; and 3) plant your roots deep in God's soil. If you establish these disciplines and embed these qualities into yourself, it will help you find peace regarding God's will for your life, along with a power that only comes from the Living Water.

John 7:38-39 (NLT) explains this living water power: "Anyone who believes in Me may come and drink! For the Scriptures declare, 'Rivers of living water will flow from his heart.' (When He said 'living water,' He was speaking of the Spirit, who would be given to everyone believing in Him. . . .)." You and I have a power greater than our natural strength. All we need to do is tap into that power and watch God *show off*. We will have a spiritual caffeine explosion when we allow the Spirit's work in our lives.

So let's control the controllable of seeking Him, walking worthy of our calling, and living out our days with a Christ-like attitude.

Reflection Questions

1. What are you doing with the second chance you have been given?

2. Do you find it easy or difficult to control the controllable of righteousness, faith, love, and endurance?

3. Through the pandemic, did you learn to be more flexible? Share how you have become more flexible.

Twelve
Refresh and Relaunch

W ell, here we are, at the last chapter of our time together. I know the process of this book has been a couple years' journey for me, and while some points have been good reminders, others have been life-changing. I hope your days are a little brighter and more joy-filled because of the changes the Lord has impressed on you. I know I am not perfect, and I can get caught in negative thinking or a complaining attitude. However, I try to not let those bouts last as long as they once did by doing my best to catch myself in the act of changing my perspective sooner rather than later. Remember, you might need to take baby steps in achieving the goals you set, but each step finds you closer to the end goal—a more positive perspective and attitude.

But let's be honest. Most of us have struggled through the COVID days in one way or another and at times have been left feeling exhausted and overwhelmed, in need of refreshing joy. Are you able to see the future with fresh eyes, or are you dragging last year's uncertainty into a new year?

Just because you have flipped the calendar to a new year, moved your location, or have shaken off a toxic relationship, you are not guaranteed change. . . or are you? Again, the answer to that question will be up to you and your perspective. As we have established through the chapters of this book, you are the only one who can choose joy, search for peace, change your mindset, and live in the certainty of God.

Although we don't know when things will feel "normal" again, we do know our lives and the way we do things have been changed. Regardless of what it looks like, we can continue to fulfill God's call and move forward. We can continue to bring joy in the lives of others. Just as the angels warned Lot, his wife, and two daughters in Genesis 19:17, we must also keep moving forward and not get stuck in the past: "Do not look behind you, and do not stay anywhere in the valley; escape to the mountains or you will be swept away." Lot's wife didn't heed the warning and looked back at what she was leaving. When she did, she was turned into a pillar of salt (v. 26). She became a permanent display of the serious consequences of disobedience and worldliness.[1]

Oh yes, we can learn from what is behind us, but we must take what we have learned and apply it to what is in front of us. The warning that hit me from Genesis 19:17 is, "Do not stay anywhere in the valley." In other words, "Don't get stuck in the low." Psalm 23:4 is a promise you will need to claim to help move you beyond the valley, "Even though

I walk through the valley of the shadow of death, I fear no evil, for You are with me; Your rod and Your staff, they comfort me." Yes, our Lord is right next to us in every step we take, and He has not given us a spirit of fear but of power, love, and a sound mind (2 Timothy 1:7). Remember what Søren Kierkegaard, a Danish theologian, philosopher, poet, social critic, and religious author said, "Life can only be understood backwards, but it must be lived forwards."

So, in order to move forward, what steps will you need to take to refresh your walk with Him and then relaunch your days ahead?

I hope the following five steps will help you focus on the importance of refreshing your walk and reset your priorities if needed.

1.   Be a good follower.

The Lord is my shepherd,
I will not be in need.
He lets me lie down in green pastures;
He leads me beside quiet waters.
He restores my soul;
He guides me in the paths of righteousness
for the sake of His name.
(Psalm 23:1-3)

The common denominator is "He." Everything referencing these verses is about Him and His leading—we are the followers: He lets us lie down, He leads, He restores, He guides. Too many times followers get a bad rap, but to be effective in ministry, we must be good followers of the one true God. Following isn't bad as long as we are following the right people or person. Jesus didn't call His disciples to be leaders; He called them to be followers. Jesus' call to follow Him is more than an invitation to pray a prayer. It is a call to lose our lives and find new life and ultimate joy in Him. . . When we truly engage with Jesus' personal invitation to follow Him, everything changes, for He is worthy of all our trust and affections. So you and I must follow Jesus every day. How do we do that? By being in the Word of God.

2.   Prioritize the Word of God.

The Law of the Lord is perfect,
restoring the soul;
the testimony of the Lord is sure,
making wise the simple.
(Psalm 19:7)

Psalm 19 tells us the Word of God restores our souls (v. 7), enlightens our eyes (v. 8), cleanses us (v. 9), is sweeter than honey (v. 10), warns us (v. 11), and provides great reward (v. 11). I recently discovered that Psalm 19 is definitely the cliff notes, or shorter version, of Psalm 119. If you need a little revival and renewal in reading the Word of God and want to reestablish the importance of God's Word, then read Psalm 119 in its entirety. You will encounter words like counselor, strength, salvation, knowledge, delight, wisdom, understanding, joy, light, awestruck, and peace.

However, the word used most frequently based on Psalm 119 is "revive" or "revival"—God's Word brings a personal revival. This type of revival will bring you back to life, wake you up, and restore your mind and days. He makes all things new, so He is continually trying to renew your thinking and bring revival to your days. He brings all things to life! Reading His Word daily will provide a spiritual reset for your day and the year ahead. Let's make being in His Word a priority and watch God reveal Himself and His will to us.

3. Embrace the nearness of God.

The Lord is near to all who call on Him,
to all who call on Him in truth.
(Psalm 145:18)

The key lies in your ability to embrace His presence by drawing near to Him. May you be encouraged by David's declaration in Psalm 27:4: "One thing I have asked from the Lord, that I shall seek: that I may dwell in the house of the Lord all the days of my life, to behold the beauty

of the Lord and to meditate in His temple." This Scripture
captures the heart and passion of David. Although he spent
countless hours tending his father's sheep and running from
King Saul, he never lost his desire for the presence of the
Lord. From the pasture to the strongholds of the wilderness,
his deepest longing was to be near to God.

Consider also the example of Jesus. He often went out
alone into the mountains to pray. He was seeking a place
of quietness—a sense of being near His Father so He could
hear that still, small voice (Luke 6:12). May this, too, be
the yearning of our hearts. Take these next few moments to
be captured by the stillness of His presence in your day. He
is a God who is near, not a far-off God (Jeremiah 23:23).

1. Discover rest

> *Be still, and know that I am God:*
> *I will be exalted among the heathen,*
> *I will be exalted in the earth.*
> (Psalm 46:10 KJV)

Rest will energize you and prepare you for what lies
ahead. Make sure to take some time for yourself. It's
okay! It's important to take care of yourself so you will be
stronger to take care of others. Remember what Psalm 23:2
says, "He lets me lie down in green pastures." The timeless
words of Corrie ten Boom have never been more applicable
in my lifetime than right now, "Never be afraid to trust an

unknown future to a known God." He's got your life in His hands. Oh, that we would entrust our days into His hands! If you need to revisit Chapter Ten, "Stop and Pick the Raspberries," for your daily reminder of rest, do it!

5. Focus your gaze.

> *But the one who joins himself to*
> *the Lord is one spirit with* Him.
> (1 Corinthians 6:17)

In the Greek, "join" (*kóllao*) means "to fasten firmly together, cleave, glue together, or cement."[2] Jesus wants us to be one with Him (John 17:21). If you are drawing life from any other source besides God, that source will not sustain you. Philippians 3:8-9 encourages us to be found in Him, "More than that, I count all things to be loss in view of the surpassing value of knowing Christ Jesus my Lord, for whom I have suffered the loss of all things, and count them mere rubbish, so that I may gain Christ, and may be found in Him." Don't you want to be found in Christ when He returns? I know I do.

You and I can be found in Him by following Him, prioritizing His Word, embracing His nearness, resting, and focusing our gaze on Him. Yes, these steps will rejuvenate a weary soul and propel us to move ahead.

Jeremiah 31:25 (NIV) tells us, 'I will refresh the weary and satisfy the faint." You can find your strength and power from Him who lives in you (Colossians 1:29). Being found in Him is greater than being found in the ways and hopes of this present world. It is He, our eternal God, who will last for all eternity.

We find a great, though unconventional, visual of what's important in life in the movie, *City Slickers.* In this film, each year three friends vacation away from their wives. One trip finds them on a mid-life crisis adventure through a cattle drive across the Southwest. On the journey, their cowboy guide, Curly, gets into a deep conversation with one of the friends, Mitch. The two talk about what the meaning of life is. Holding up one finger, Curly shares how there is *one thing* in life, and it's up to each of us to find out what that one purpose is. For Mitch, he found the true meaning of life and what genuinely matters in a raging river, saving a baby calf.

Can't we relate to this? Don't we each desire to truly understand what our purpose and the importance in life is? Thankfully, as believers in Jesus Christ, that purpose is crystal clear—to know Jesus. When we have Christ, we have everything. He is that one thing that is satisfying, but we must seek it. Jesus said this about Mary in Luke 10:42: 'But only one thing is necessary, for Mary has chosen the good part, which shall not be taken away from her." That one thing was Mary sitting at the feet of Jesus listening to

His Word (Luke 10:39) and being found in Him. Her desire to be close to her Savior overrode the cares of the day.

May we pursue this one thing—to seek Him above ourselves. By dwelling in His presence, beholding His beauty and meditating on His Word, we'll find ourselves walking our faith journey towards this truth and unlocking principles to a fulfilling and fruitful life.

So, what steps will you take to move forward and allow God to refresh and relaunch your days? Isaiah 43:18-19 tells us, "Do not call to mind the former things, or consider things of the past. Behold, I am going to do something new, now it will spring up; will you not be aware of it? I will even make a roadway in the wilderness, rivers in the desert."

Will you embrace the new adventures and opportunities God brings your way with an open mind and willing heart? Will you wait patiently for the future buffaloes God may be preparing you for? Ephesians 2:10 is a good reminder that God has all things in control, "For we are His workmanship, created in Christ Jesus for good works, which God prepared beforehand so that we would walk in them." Your days are in His hands, and it is His timing you need to embrace. Won't you trust that He has a plan for your life (Jeremiah 29:11) and give Him full access to your life and day? Yes, each day and year will bring highs, lows, and buffaloes. Watch for the blessings that come each day and be grateful for the surprises.

- Enjoy the highs, for they are from God.

- Accept the lows, for they are allowed from God, too.

- Enjoy the buffaloes that keep you watching for the Godwinks from God—those special divine surprises that brighten your day.

My hope through this book is that you will appreciate the great highs throughout your days, learn from the lows you experience, and be in awe of the buffaloes God blesses you with. And, as you close out each day, you will see God's hand upon your life and be grateful for His divine plan as you journey to your eternal destination.

Reflection Questions

1. Share what you have learned through reading this book—the reminders and the changes.

2. Which of the five areas to refresh your days do you need to implement into your life: become a better follower, prioritize God's Word, discover rest, experience the nearness of God, or change your focus?

3. What steps will you take to move forward and allow God to refresh and relaunch your days?

Notes

Chapter One

1. Mark Batterson, *Win the Day: 7 Daily Habits to Help You Stress Less & Accomplish More* (Colorado Springs: Multnomah, 2020, audio book).

2. Jon Gordon, *The Shark and the Goldfish: Positive Ways to Thrive During Waves of Change* (Hoboken, NJ: Wiley, 2009, p. 25).

3. Brennan Manning, *Ruthless Trust: The Ragamuffin's Path to God* (Harper Collins e-Books, 2010).

4. Excerpted from WHISPER. Copyright © 2017 by Mark Batterson. Published by Multnomah, an imprint of Penguin Random House LLC.

Chapter Two

1. Oswald Chambers, July 28 Daily Reading from *My Utmost for His Highest* (Nashville: Thomas Nelson, 1993).

2. Mark Batterson, *Do It for a Day: How to Make or Break Any Habit in 30 Days* (Colorado Springs: Multnomah, 2021, audio book).

3. Gary Martin, "'Pull Yourself up by Your Bootstraps' - the Meaning and Origin of This Phrase," Phrasefinder, 2019, www.phrases.org.uk/meanings/pull-yourself-up-by-your-bootstraps.html.

4. Oswald Chambers, June 9 Daily Reading from *My Utmost for His Highest* (Nashville: Thomas Nelson, 1993).

5. Ibid (August 2).

Chapter Four

1. Anders, *Holman New Testament Commentary*, 327.

2. G4024 - perizónnymi - *Strong's Greek Lexicon* (nasb95)," *Blue Letter Bible*, Web. 5 Jan. 2022, https://www.blueletterbible.org/lexicon/g4024/nasb95/mgnt/0-1/

Chapter Seven:

1. GotQuestions.org. "Home: What Is the Significance of the Olive Tree in the Bible?" *GotQuestions.org*, 25 Apr. 2019, www.gotquestions.org/olive-tree-Bible.html.

2. Joel Dorman, et al. "Growing Old with Life (Psalm 92:12-15)," *Life Meets Theology*, 1 Dec. 2014, lifemeetstheology.com/2014/12/03/growing-old-with-life-psalm-9212-15/.

Chapter Eight

1. John Gordon, *The Positive Dog: A Fable about Changing Your Attitude to Be Your Best* (Hoboken, NJ: Wiley, 2012).

Chapter Nine

1. Jackson-Ga, "The Word 'If' in the Bible," *Google Answers*, Google, 28 Apr. 2006, http://answers. google.com/answers/threadview/id/723790.html.

Chapter Ten

1. "H7503 - RĀPÂ - Strong's Hebrew LEXICON (NASB20)," *Blue Letter Bible*, www.blueletterbible. org/lexicon/h7503/nasb20/wlc/0-1/.

2. CSB Tony Evans Study Bible (Nashville: Holman Bible Publishers, 2019), 1254.

Chapter Twelve

1. *CSB Tony Evans Study Bible* (Nashville: Holman Bible Publishers, 2019), 23.

2. "G2853 - kóllao- Strong's Hebrew LEXICON (NASB95)." *Blue Letter Bible*, www.blueletterbible. org/lexicon/g2853/nasb95/mgnt/0-1/.

Jessie Seneca

Jessie and her husband, John, live in Bethlehem, Pennsylvania, and have been married since 1985. They have two daughters and two wonderful sons-in-law. Jessie is enjoying being a Mimi. Most days, you can find Jessie walking her two furry friends, Murphy and Baxter, or playing with her grandchildren.

Jessie is a national speaker, author, leadership trainer, and the founder of More of Him Ministries, SHE Leads leadership conference, and The Real Mom conference. She also works with LifeWay as one of their YOU Lead trainers. She has a passion for helping women experience God's Word for themselves as she encourages them to move into a "wholehearted" lifestyle, one devoted fully to God. To learn more about Jessie and her ministry, visit www.moreofhimministries.org.

Order Info

For autographed books, bulk order discounts,
or to schedule speaking engagements, contact:

Jessie Seneca
jessie.seneca@gmail.com
610.216.2730

To order any of Jessie's books, visit
www.MoreofHimMinistries.org

Also available from your favorite bookstore
Like us on Facebook

The Secret Is Out

Learn it. Live it. Pass it on.

Did you know that God has a secret? One day, while Jessie Seneca was reading Colossians 1:27 in the New Living Translation (NLT), she saw it. There it was, God's secret: "Christ lives in you. This gives you assurance of sharing in His glory." Once you know it, you will never be the same. You can enter into a wholehearted relationship with the supreme and all-sufficient Christ.

This study features five weeks of personal, daily assignments and six weekly group sessions with DVD (available separately). As this study guides you into a deeper relationship with your heavenly Father and Savior, Jesus Christ, you will be grounded in the truth of Christ, the person of Christ, and the power of Christ. You will be challenged in your everyday relationships—in the home, workplace, and church. Read and study the short yet compelling and powerful letter of Colossians. When you are finished studying it, you will not only want to learn the secret for yourself, but live it out and pass it on. A companion DVD and audio CD are available for this title.

Road Trip

A personal journey through life's detours and pit stops

Are you "living life" and wondering where all your plans went, only to realize that God's plans were always your plans and you just didn't see it? Road Trip is Jessie's journey in her battle with Cushing's Syndrome, a life-threatening disease. Her story looks back at her ride through the ups and downs of her struggles, how God brought her through them victoriously, and how He is using her experiences for His purposes.

This book encourages you to see God's big picture in your own life and appreciate the detours and pit stops along the way that will help make you stronger and live a more purpose-filled life. Road Trip includes a study guide for personal reflection or group discussion.

Joseph

A Life of Rejection, Resilience and Respect

A re you in need of a "pick me up" adjustment? Maybe you have been touched by rejection, shattered dreams, or are presently going through hard times. Studying the life of Joseph will help you understand the relevance of Joseph's experiences— from rejection and hurt to God's sovereignty, every step of the way. As you read and study about this most popular and beloved Bible character, you will find your own place in the journey and see God's plan fulfilled in and through your life. You will come out on the other side with hope, encouragement and compassion. This study features six weeks of personal, daily assignments and seven weekly group sessions with DVD teaching (available separately).

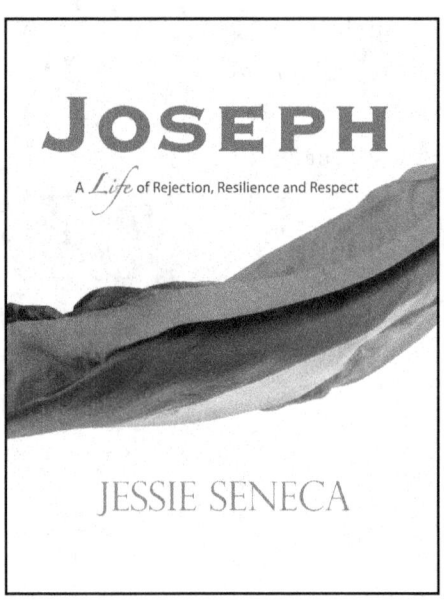

Friendship

Sisters for a Journey

Friendship, Sisters for a Journey will help you discover the secret to authentic friendship through meaningful and purposeful relationships. Sometimes it might look a little messy and other times glorious, but God uses all styles and seasons of friendships to grow and stretch us into better friends, sisters, mothers, daughters, aunts, grandmothers, and any other roles we fill.

Jessie Seneca
Foreword by Gwen Smith, *Girlfriends in God*

52 Promises from God

A Devotional Journal, Reflections to Sooth Your Soul

Longing for a soul soothing devotional that will remind you of God's faithfulness? 52 Promises from God will satisfy the depths of your heart as you are reminded of God's goodness. At your own pace, soak in these Biblical truths and spend time reflecting on His promises in your life. This beautifully designed hardcover devotional will jumpstart your day with deep encouragement and steadfast assurance that God fulfills the promises He made you through His word.

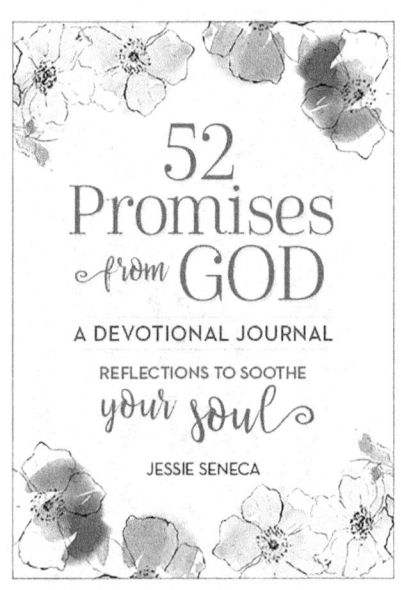

More of Jesus Less of Me

Principles for Fruitful Living

This book helps readers unfold what it means to set our selfish desires aside to deeply desire God and pursue a God-centered lifestyle-one fully devoted to Him. Surely, this is not an easy task, but it's a desire worth seeking and searching for until the end of our days.

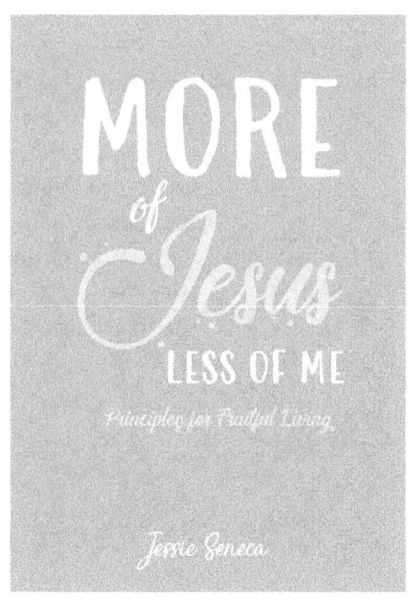

Raising Girls

Diaper to Diamond

Mom. Three simple letters, when put together, give you a life-changing title. Raising a daughter is one of the greatest blessings God can give, and He chose you for the unique role to teach His ways and pass down biblical womanhood to future generations. No one can do it quite like you, Mom! While writing *Raising Girls: Diaper to Diamond,* Jessie Seneca had one question at the forefront of her mind, "What do I wish I could tell the younger me?" Jessie, who has raised two daughters, draws truth and guidance from Scripture, personal experience and practical insights from other moms. She doesn't claim to have all the answers. Like most of us, she has made mistakes along the way, but her continued desire is to see girls develop into responsible, faith-filled women. With discussion questions at the conclusion of each chapter, you'll feel empowered with thought-provoking conversations addressing a wide variety of topics such as dating, mean girls, self-image, perfectionism, a father's role and much

more. Oh, and don't forget about that de-parenting stage we all experience as our daughters leave the safety of our homes to conquer the world in front of them. May you rise up and embrace this special calling of motherhood!

RAISING
GIRLS
Diaper to Diamond

Jessie Seneca
Foreword by Arlene Pellicane
author of *31 Days to Becoming a Happy Mom*

Abound

A Call to Purposeful Servant LEADERSHIP

The Call • The Walk • The Leap • The Team
4 manageable chapters for the busy leader

In this motivational book, Jessie Seneca unpacks your call to a Person, a Purpose, a Passion, and a People, encouraging you to walk with intentionality before God and your team—always abounding in the work of the Lord.

Blending practical insight from noted leaders within their field, Jessie brings wisdom from her own successes and struggles through her real-life experiences, opportunities, desires, and dreams.

The weekly self-development exercises will empower you to take the next step in fulfilling your call and enlisting other like-minded leaders to join your ventures, opportunities, desires, and dreams.

Choose the approach that fits you in your season of leadership:

- Read the book for yourself.

- Read the book for yourself and complete the weekly self-development exercises.

- Read the book with your team.

- Read the book with your team and complete the weekly self-development exercises.

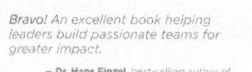

Bravo! An excellent book helping leaders build passionate teams for greater impact.

— Dr. Hans Finzel, best-selling author of *The Top Ten Mistakes Leaders Make*

A call to purposeful
servant LEADERSHIP

JESSIE SENECA

This is not just a journey but a pursuit to abound in the work of the Lord. Embrace your call. Walk it out with strength. Take the leap and never stop dreaming.

www.ingramcontent.com/pod-product-compliance
Lightning Source LLC
Chambersburg PA
CBHW061155120626
46546CB00005B/2069